Paradox Theory

By Saechan Jung

Copyright © 2025 by Saechan Jung

All rights reserved.

Table of Contents

PROLOGUE 1

THE PARADOX OF CONTROL 3

    THE MORE YOU TRY TO CONTROL, THE MORE YOU LOSE IT 3
    WHEN LETTING GO BRINGS MORE POWER 6
    ORDER FEEDS CHAOS 10
    THE COST OF PREDICTABILITY 12

THE VALUE OF A PERSON 17

    SOCIAL CURRENCY 17
    YOUR PERSONALITY IS NOT ENOUGH 20
    MEASURED BY OUTPUT, DEFINED BY NUMBERS 23
    WHO ARE YOU WITHOUT A MIRROR? 26

THE PARADOX OF PROGRESS 30

    THE FASTER WE ADVANCE, THE EMPTIER WE FEEL 30
    INNOVATION SOLVES EVERYTHING, UNTIL IT DOESN'T 33
    THE FASTER WE MOVE, THE LESS WE ARRIVE 37
    SUCCESS THAT FEELS WRONG 40

THE PARADOX OF ORIGINALITY 44

    THE DESIRE TO BE DIFFERENT 44
    THE IDENTITY COPY LOOP 46
    THE ECHO CHAMBER OF CREATIVITY 49
    INSPIRATION OR INHERITANCE? 51

THE FREEDOM IN LIMITATION 55

    THE PRISON OF TOO MUCH FREEDOM 55
    WHY CONSTRAINTS SPARK CREATIVITY 59
    SAYING NO AS A FORM OF POWER 63
    YOU CAN DO ANYTHING, SO YOU DO NOTHING 66

THE SPOTLIGHT EFFECT 71

    THE ECHO OF JUDGMENT THAT WAS NEVER SPOKEN 71
    SHAME IN A WORLD THAT FORGETS 74
    INVISIBLE EYES, VISIBLE PRESSURE 77

- The Audience That Got It Wrong 86

THE HEDONIC TREADMILL 94

- The Chase That Never Ends 94
- The Happiness That Never Stays 102
- The Illusion of Arrival 110
- Trapped in the Upgrade Loop 118

THE SAFETY THAT MAKES YOU UNSAFE 126

- The Shield That Shatters 126
- The Fragility of Overprotection 135
- When Precaution Becomes the Threat 144
- Collapse of care 151

THE FATE THAT WAS CHOSEN 156

- The Prophecy That Wrote Itself 156
- The Choice That Was Never Yours 164
- Fighting Fate, Fulfilling It 169
- The Fork That Never Split 173

THE TRUTH THAT CHANGES NOTHING 177

- The Revelation That Left Everything Intact 177
- The Burden of Knowing 179
- The Clarity That Closed the Door 185
- The Unmoving Truth 189
- So what does it take to move an unmoving truth? 194

MORALITY THAT DIVIDES 195

- The Right Side That Refuses to Listen 195
- The Good That Turns Against Itself 197
- The Principles That Destroy Peace 200
- The Belief That Cannot Be Questioned 203

FINAL NOTE 206

ABOUT ME 207

Prologue

What Is a Paradox?

A paradox is a situation where two facts, ideas, or outcomes contradict each other and yet both remain true.

It is when trying to hold on makes something slip away faster. When freedom creates emptiness instead of fulfillment. When safety becomes the very thing that makes you more vulnerable. Paradoxes are not errors or illusions. They are real, measurable patterns and they often sit at the center of human behavior, relationships, and entire systems.

They are the moments when logic fails, but life continues.

A paradox is not just an idea that feels confusing. It is a structure that forces you to think differently. You cannot solve a paradox by picking a side. You solve it by noticing the tension and learning to think in two directions at once.

Most people are uncomfortable with that. We are taught to want clear answers, linear steps, and consistent outcomes. But the world does not run on consistency. It runs on contradictions that do not cancel each other out. They coexist, and they shape everything from personal struggles to cultural patterns.

This book is about those contradictions. The ones that don't go away just because we understand them. The ones that live in plain sight, inside our decisions, beliefs, and habits.

To explore paradoxes is to study how people try to control the uncontrollable, how comfort can create weakness, how logic leads people into failure, and how progress sometimes feels like loss. It is not just about noticing that life is complicated, it is about recognizing that some things only make sense once you stop trying to force them to.

Each chapter in this book will focus on a different paradox, not to explain it away, but to expose what it reveals. Because paradoxes do not block truth. They point to it. They show us where the easy answers end.

And there is no better place to begin than with the paradox that most people live by without realizing it, the belief that control brings power.

The Paradox of Control

The More You Try to Control, the More You Lose It

Control is something nearly every person desires. From the small details of a daily routine to the major decisions that shape a life, humans naturally seek structure, predictability, and power over their environments. We crave a sense of agency, a reassurance that our choices matter, that we can determine the direction of our own lives. Control feels like safety. It feels like clarity. And yet, when people cling to it too tightly, something strange happens. Things begin to unravel. Plans fall apart, relationships strain, anxiety rises, and in the pursuit of control, chaos often follows.

This is the paradox: the more you try to control, the more you lose it.

Consider the workplace. A manager who micromanages their employees might believe they are improving productivity or ensuring quality. They monitor every task, question every decision, and demand frequent updates. In the short term, this behavior might create the illusion of efficiency. But in reality, it fosters resentment, kills creativity, and reduces morale. Employees begin to disengage, innovation stalls, and the workplace becomes toxic. The manager wanted control, but by forcing it, they lost what really mattered, trust, respect, and sustainable output.

Now shift this to personal relationships. Think of a parent who tries to control every part of their child's life, from what they eat, to who they are friends with, to what career they should pursue. That child may comply at first. They may follow instructions, meet expectations, and aim to please. But eventually, tension builds.

Rebellion surfaces. The child begins to lie, push boundaries, or cut off communication altogether. The parent, in trying to keep their child safe, has driven them away. Their grip became a wedge. The more control they exerted, the more disconnection they created.

The same principle applies to personal habits and routines. Some people structure every moment of their day. Wake at exactly 5:00 AM. Eat the same breakfast. Plan every hour. Set detailed goals. Build systems. In theory, it sounds disciplined, focused, and productive. But when even the smallest interruption throws the day into disarray, when deviation sparks guilt or anxiety, it reveals a fragility. These routines were meant to give order, but they now control the person. Instead of creating freedom, control has created a cage.

Why does this paradox exist? It has to do with the nature of reality itself. The world is full of unpredictable, moving parts. People change their minds. Markets fluctuate. Accidents happen. Emotions surge. There are too many variables. Total control is an illusion. Life cannot be tamed completely, and those who refuse to accept this truth tend to suffer more. The harder you squeeze, the more things slip through your fingers.

But there is a deeper layer too. Control often stems from fear. Fear of failure. Fear of loss. Fear of uncertainty. When people are afraid, they tighten their grip. They try to control outcomes, control people, control everything. But fear based control does not lead to strength. It leads to exhaustion, rigidity, and a kind of internal collapse. People who operate from fear may appear powerful, but inside, they are anxious and unstable.

What is the alternative? It is not giving up. It is not apathy or detachment. It is something more balanced, acceptance. Acceptance is not passivity. It does not mean you stop making decisions or setting goals. It means recognizing what is within your control and what is not. It means acting without obsession, guiding without force, and adapting when life shifts unexpectedly.

In psychology, this idea is captured by the concept of "locus of control." A person with an internal locus believes they can influence their life through effort, choices, and habits. A person with an external locus believes they are at the mercy of fate, luck, or other people. But even this model has its limits. Sometimes, internal control can tip into delusion, while external control can become an excuse. The healthiest approach sits somewhere in between, where effort meets flexibility, and ambition meets humility.

The paradox of control becomes clearer when you look at leadership. The best leaders do not cling to power. They empower others. They delegate, listen, and remain open to feedback. Their authority is not derived from domination but from clarity, trust, and a shared vision. Ironically, by relinquishing control, they gain influence. They create movements, not just machines.

The same applies to creative work. Writers, artists, and musicians often describe the moment when they stop trying to force an idea and instead allow it to unfold naturally. The creative process flourishes when tension is released. When someone chases perfection or obsesses over every line, the work often feels flat or forced. But when they let go, when they trust the process, something genuine emerges.

Even in finance and investing, the paradox shows itself. Those who try to perfectly time the market, constantly tweak their portfolios, or chase every trend often underperform. Meanwhile, those who create a long term plan, accept short term volatility, and avoid emotional reactions tend to see better results. Letting go of the illusion of total control actually improves outcomes.

There is also a moral element to control. When people try to control others, their beliefs, their identities, their choices, it becomes an act of domination. Throughout history, entire societies have been damaged by the desire to control others. Oppressive regimes, rigid ideologies, and toxic systems are all born from the refusal to let people be free. And they all eventually collapse.

So what does this mean on a personal level? It means you must examine your own relationship with control. Where do you hold on too tightly? Where is your grip hurting you more than it is helping? Are you trying to control people, outcomes, or feelings that you cannot, and should not, manage? Are you addicted to certainty in a world that was never built to provide it?

Letting go does not mean you become careless. It means you become clear. Clear about your values, your intentions, and your place in the bigger picture. You still steer your ship, but you do not try to control the wind and waves. You learn to adjust your sails.

The paradox of control teaches that freedom comes not from controlling everything, but from knowing what to control and what to release. It is a lesson in wisdom, in strength, and in peace.

And sometimes, when you let go of the need to dominate life, life finally begins to move with you, not against you.

When Letting Go Brings More Power

Letting go is often misunderstood. People associate it with weakness, apathy, or failure. The phrase "let it go" is typically offered as a shallow comfort or a way to dismiss someone's frustration. But in truth, the act of letting go requires more strength than most people realize. And in many cases, it leads not to loss, but to something greater, clarity, influence, and even power. This is the paradox.

You gain more control by surrendering your need for it.

In life, much of what people fight to hold on to does not serve them. They hold on to outdated plans, broken relationships, impossible standards, or goals that no longer reflect who they are. The tighter they cling, the more trapped they feel. They become reactive instead of responsive. Defensive instead of curious. Rigid instead of adaptive.

Nowhere is this more visible than in leadership. The most respected leaders are those who are not afraid to step back and allow others to lead. They understand that control, when hoarded, shrinks the potential of a team. But when shared wisely, it multiplies results. They let go of ego. They trust people to make decisions. They remain present, but not invasive. They are not afraid to say, "You do not need me for this." And that trust builds loyalty.

In relationships, the power of letting go becomes even more obvious. People often hold on to others out of fear, fear of being alone, of not being loved, or of not finding something better. They try to control the dynamic by overanalyzing every message, trying to predict the other person's reactions, or suppressing their own needs just to keep the peace. But this form of control erodes authenticity. The relationship becomes performance instead of connection.

The people who are most magnetic are often the ones who are not desperately trying to be liked. They are not controlling how they are seen. They are not chasing approval. And because they are not gripped by fear, they are free to be themselves, and that confidence draws others in. They let go of the need to be perfect, and in doing so, become more attractive, more trustworthy, and more comfortable to be around.

Letting go is also crucial in the face of failure. Many people are haunted by mistakes, regrets, or things that did not go according to plan. They replay conversations, imagine different outcomes, or stay stuck in cycles of blame. They think that if they hold on long enough, they can rewrite what happened. But they cannot. The past is fixed. And the only real control lies in how one moves forward.

People who grow quickly are not those who avoid failure, but those who refuse to be owned by it. They let go of what cannot be changed. They extract the lesson and release the weight. That act of release is not passive, it is active, conscious, and liberating. It is a reclaiming of energy.

Even in mental health, letting go plays a critical role. Obsessive thoughts, perfectionism, and chronic anxiety are often symptoms of the mind clinging too tightly to certainty or control. The need to predict everything, fix everything, or prepare for every possible outcome becomes a prison. What provides relief is not more planning or more control, it is surrender. The ability to sit with discomfort, to breathe through uncertainty, and to say, "I cannot know, and that is okay."

Letting go is not a single event. It is a skill, a practice, and often a painful one. It means facing discomfort. It means admitting that some things are outside your influence. It means grieving the illusion of control you once depended on. And it means learning to trust, trust the process, trust others, and in many ways, trust yourself.

There is a paradox here, too. People think they will lose their identity if they let go of certain expectations or habits. But in reality, identity often becomes clearer when you stop trying to define it so rigidly. By releasing the image you are trying to maintain, you create space for something real to emerge. What is authentic is often discovered in the absence of pressure.

Letting go does not mean you stop caring. It means you stop forcing. You still act with intention. You still work hard. But you stop trying to manipulate every outcome. You stop gripping life with white knuckles and start holding it with open hands.

This mindset shift is especially powerful in long term goals. Whether someone is building a business, creating a body of work, or trying to change a part of their life, the process is never linear. Obstacles come. Motivation fades. Progress stalls. People who succeed are often the ones who let go of rigid timelines and narrow definitions of success. They stay flexible. They adapt. And because they are not attached to a specific picture, they are more able to see new opportunities as they appear.

In negotiation, this principle is called "having a strong walk away." The person who is willing to walk away from the deal often has the most leverage. They are not desperate. They are not emotionally entangled. They have options, and they know it. That confidence shifts the power dynamic. Ironically, the person who cares less about winning often ends up winning.

In parenting, the shift from control to guidance becomes essential as children grow. What works at age five does not work at age fifteen. Parents who let go of the illusion that they can control every aspect of their child's development begin to cultivate respect and open communication. They become mentors, not dictators. And their children grow into adults who can think independently.

In philosophy and spirituality, letting go has always been a cornerstone. From Buddhism's concept of non attachment to Stoicism's focus on what is within your power, wisdom traditions across the world have long understood this paradox. The path to peace is not paved with total control, it is paved with awareness, humility, and release.

And finally, letting go allows for something beautiful, surprise. Life is filled with unexpected moments, connections, and breakthroughs. But they rarely appear when you are gripping too tightly to your plan. They come when you are open. When you have cleared the space. When you have said, without bitterness or fear, "Let us see what happens."

Order Feeds Chaos

We are taught to organize our lives. Calendars, routines, and expectations give us structure. We make schedules, set alarms, categorize tasks, and create systems to keep everything in order. But underneath that appearance of structure is a quieter, less discussed reality, the more tightly we try to impose order, the more fragile everything becomes.

There is a reason that overly managed environments often fail when exposed to pressure. A perfectly timed life leaves no space for unpredictability, and when the unexpected finally arrives, it feels catastrophic. A canceled meeting, a sudden bill, an illness, a rejection, these small disruptions feel larger when everything else has been so carefully controlled. The mind that expects order all the time struggles the most when chaos enters the room.

Ironically, it is in our efforts to remove chaos that we often multiply it. A company with too many rules creates bottlenecks. A family with too many expectations builds resentment. A government with too many controls weakens trust. Order becomes so thick that it turns into confusion, and those living within it lose the ability to adapt. The goal was clarity, but what results is constraint.

Think of the systems we admire the most, those that can bend without breaking. They are not strict or rigid. They are adaptive. They allow for fluctuations. That is why chaos, in moderation, is not a threat. It is a signal. It reveals where the structure was too weak, too inflexible, too dependent on everything going exactly according to plan.

It is not that order is bad. Order is necessary. The problem arises when order becomes absolute. When we try to control every outcome, we begin to fear any result we did not plan. And when that fear grows, we act out of panic. We overcorrect. We overthink. We micromanage. The more we chase control, the more out of control we actually feel.

This paradox is everywhere. In parenting, the more rules are enforced without trust, the more children rebel. In work, the more meetings and metrics dominate the culture, the more burnout spreads. In relationships, the more you try to control another person, the more distant they become. And within yourself, the more pressure you place on being perfect, the more mistakes you begin to make.

Chaos is not a flaw in the system. It is part of the system. It tests what works and what does not. It challenges our designs. And it is only when we allow space for it that we begin to build things that last. A life without chaos is not a sign of success. It is a warning that something may be missing. Because a life that cannot handle disorder is not truly stable. It is simply untested.

When we let go of the obsession with order, something shifts. We become more creative. We improvise. We problem solve. We start asking better questions instead of rigidly defending our assumptions. We gain flexibility. And in that flexibility, we find a deeper kind of strength. The kind that does not panic when plans change. The kind that endures.

Letting go does not mean you are giving up. It means you are trusting yourself to respond to life instead of controlling every detail ahead of time. It means understanding that chaos will come no matter how much you prepare, so you might as well prepare to respond rather than control.

The world is not a puzzle that can be solved once and for all. It is a river. It moves. It flows. It bends around corners you cannot see yet. And if your life is built too tightly, it will crack under pressure. But if it has room to shift, it will survive the storms.

So order your life, but do not fear chaos. Build systems, but leave space for messiness. Make plans, but know they will break. And when they do, trust that you will still be standing. Because sometimes, the strongest structure is the one that knows how to fall and rebuild.

The Cost of Predictability

There is comfort in knowing what comes next. People crave routine. It allows for structure, a sense of control, a way to navigate a chaotic world without constantly falling apart. From childhood, we are conditioned to think that predictability is safety. That following the well paved road will protect us from failure, shame, or regret. And in many ways, it does. But there is a cost, one that is rarely acknowledged until it is too late to reverse it.

The routines we build become the cages we live in. Predictability may feel like stability, but it also quietly erodes our sense of agency. When life becomes a series of expected steps, taken not because we chose them but because they were handed to us, we stop noticing that we never explored the alternative. We do not question what we could have become had we taken the harder, messier, less certain path. Because uncertainty feels dangerous. It threatens the image of security we spent so long constructing. And so we stay predictable, even when it dulls us.

In most people's lives, there is a timeline that looks eerily similar. School, graduation, college, job, marriage, house, family, retirement. Within this formula lies the illusion of freedom. It looks like a choice, but it is not. Most of those choices were offered on someone else's terms. They were shaped by economic structures, social expectations, and deeply ingrained fears. The result is a predictable life, but not necessarily a fulfilling one.

It is not that there is anything wrong with a traditional path. The problem begins when that path is walked mindlessly. Predictability becomes expensive when it prevents us from asking difficult questions, when it trades curiosity for comfort, when it replaces risk with routine. We lose the part of ourselves that wonders, that doubts, that rebels, that dreams of something else entirely. And that is not a small price.

Even innovation suffers under predictability. The most influential ideas did not come from people who stayed on script. They came from those who questioned the script itself. Predictability keeps systems functioning, but it does not evolve them. Change, by nature, is disruptive. And most people have been taught that disruption is dangerous. So instead of creating, they conform.

The cost of predictability also appears in the way people define success. If success is simply achieving what was expected, then success is no longer inspiring. It becomes mechanical. Graduate with a good GPA. Get a good job. Save a set percentage of your income. Buy a home by a certain age. These are measurable outcomes, and they are often achievable. But what do they mean if they were never personal goals to begin with? Whose idea of success are we really chasing?

Predictability makes life quieter, but not richer. It can eliminate chaos, but it also silences passion. A predictable life is often a safe one, but it can also be a deeply lonely one. Not because there are no people around, but because there is no version of you that feels fully alive in it. There is no tension, no struggle that leads to insight, no moment where the ground breaks open and forces you to confront what matters most.

The irony is that many people wake up decades later realizing they followed all the rules, did everything right, and still feel incomplete. They are not unhappy because they failed. They are unhappy because they never deviated. They never took the wrong turn that might have led to a new city, a new idea, or a new version of themselves. They were predictable, and that predictability eventually became invisible. No one questioned it. Not even them.

This kind of life creates a unique form of regret. Not the regret of failure, but the regret of never trying something different. The regret of being so focused on getting things right that you never stopped to ask whether they were worth getting right in the first place. It is the kind of regret that surfaces at odd moments, in the middle of the night or in the silence of an empty room, when the routine breaks and you are left wondering what you missed.

Predictability also influences relationships. Many people settle not because they lack options, but because they are told that settling is mature. That passion fades, that commitment is more important than excitement, that you should choose the steady option over the uncertain one. But choosing someone out of predictability instead of connection is not a virtue. It is a slow erosion of intimacy. And eventually, it creates a life where you are surrounded by people, yet still feel alone.

The same logic applies to careers. People stay in jobs they dislike for decades because they fear instability. They convince themselves that a paycheck matters more than purpose, that consistency is more valuable than growth. While that is sometimes true for survival, it is often not true for fulfillment. Predictability in work creates burnout just as quickly as chaos. It drains your energy in small, quiet ways until you forget what it feels like to be fully engaged.

The paradox is clear. Predictability can give us what we want in the short term, but take from us what we need in the long term. It protects us from failure, but it also shields us from discovery. It gives us peace, but at the cost of depth. It makes us efficient, but not imaginative.

Some people argue that predictability is necessary for a functioning society. And to some extent, they are right. Not everyone can afford to chase dreams or question routines. But even within limited options, there is always room for questioning. There is always space to think differently, to imagine something new, to carve out even a small piece of unpredictability in a world that values sameness.

Predictability is expensive not because it demands our money, but because it demands our imagination. It asks us to believe that the most efficient life is the most worthwhile one. It teaches us that boredom is safer than failure. It whispers that comfort is the same as contentment. And over time, we stop asking for more, not because we do not want it, but because we forget it was ever possible.

The cost of predictability is not just missed opportunity. It is a missed identity. It is a life where you never discover your full capacity because you never had to stretch it. It is a story written by others, followed without edit, and closed without resistance.

To live a life that matters, you have to be willing to disrupt it. You have to ask whether the road you are on was chosen, or simply assigned. You have to be willing to risk instability for authenticity. And most importantly, you have to recognize that comfort, while sweet, can also be a trap.

A predictable life is not necessarily a bad one. But if you never question it, it might not be yours.

The Value of a Person

Social Currency

In the world we live in, the value of a person is rarely measured in who they are. It is measured in what they offer. Not emotionally, not morally, but socially. What circles do they move in? What title follows their name? What do they bring to the table when there is no dinner, only status?

This is the paradox of social currency. You are told growing up that everyone is equal. That every person has worth, no matter their background or looks or bank account. But then you grow older and realize that worth has conditions. Society does not reward everyone equally. It rewards influence, connections, fame, and appearance. And if you do not have these things, your voice can disappear into silence.

You can walk into a room and be ignored, not because of your ideas, but because of your clothes. You can make a brilliant point in a meeting and be dismissed, only for someone with a better reputation to say the same thing and get applause. It is not always intentional. But it is real. It is the silent economy of attention.

In a world obsessed with image, your presence becomes a currency. The way you look, the number of followers you have, the confidence in your walk. These things shape how people treat you, whether they admit it or not. And over time, that treatment starts to shape how you see yourself.

There are people who have worked harder than anyone else, with more skill and more heart, but they are overlooked because they do not fit the mold. They do not know the right people. They did not go to the right school. They are not charming enough, or polished enough, or strategic enough. And so their value gets discounted, not based on what they are, but on how they are perceived.

This is why the concept of "networking" matters so much. It is not just about who you know, but who knows you, and more importantly, what they think when they hear your name. That reaction becomes your social credit score. People will lend you opportunities, trust, and time based on that invisible number, and you do not always get to control how it is calculated.

You can be kind, honest, and capable, but if someone more influential says otherwise, that opinion will weigh heavier than your truth. And this is what makes social value so fragile. It is not earned the same way for everyone, and it can disappear faster than it appeared. A rumor, a mistake, or a moment of weakness can tear it down.

People will say, "Just be yourself." But what they really mean is, "Be yourself as long as it fits the image we like." Authenticity is celebrated until it makes others uncomfortable. Honesty is praised until it challenges someone more powerful. And uniqueness is encouraged only within the boundaries of what is profitable.

There is a strange contradiction in how we define popularity. The most followed people online are not necessarily the wisest, or the kindest, or even the most talented. They are the most visible. And in a world where visibility equals value, people start trading their time, identity, and integrity just to be seen.

Some will pretend to be something they are not because that version is more acceptable. Others will stay quiet in rooms where they could speak, just because they feel their words will not carry weight. And slowly, the true self gets buried under layers of performance.

But the danger is not just in being overlooked. It is in believing that you do not matter unless others decide that you do. When the approval of strangers becomes the mirror you use to measure your own worth, you begin to chase their validation like oxygen.

This creates another paradox. The more you need others to value you, the less you value yourself. Because their standards change. One day, you are trending. The next, you are forgotten. If your worth is tied to that, then your identity becomes unstable, swinging between highs and lows that are never in your control.

The problem is not ambition. It is not wrong to want to be respected or recognized. The problem is how we are taught to earn it. Not through growth or learning or meaning, but through surface impressions. It tells people that their value is something to be proven, not something they already have.

And that message becomes foggy when applied to young people. Because it teaches them that they need to brand themselves like a product. That they need to fit into a template before they can be seen. That their face must match a trend, their voice must follow a script, and their life must look a certain way to be accepted.

What if the real value of a person cannot be seen at a glance? What if it is found in things that take time to notice? Like the way someone shows up when no one else does. The consistency in their words. The calm they bring into a room. These qualities are not loud, but they are real. And yet, in a world of quick impressions, they are often missed.

The truth is, every person carries a value that numbers cannot calculate. But that truth is hidden under the noise. And if society keeps teaching people to trade themselves for attention, we are going to lose the very things that make us human.

That is the paradox of social currency. The more we try to prove our worth to others, the more disconnected we become from the things that actually make us worthy. And until we stop measuring people like products, we will keep walking past the best parts of each other without ever seeing them.

Your Personality Is Not Enough

There was a time when being kind, thoughtful, or loyal was enough to define a person. Those were considered traits of value. You could walk into a room and leave an impression because of how you carried yourself, how you made others feel. Today, that kind of worth feels less relevant. It has been replaced by a different kind of scorekeeping, one where who you are matters less than what you do, how fast you move, and how visible your success is to others.

You can be the most genuine person in the world, but if you do not have anything to show for it, the world does not seem to care. You could have the best intentions, the strongest work ethic, and the kindest heart, but if your resume does not look a certain way, or your bank account is not high enough, or your profile is not impressive enough, then it is like none of it matters.

It is not that personality is meaningless. It is that the world has placed it further down the list of priorities. We live in an age of performance. People are branding themselves like companies, selling their identity like products. If you are not interesting, entertaining, or productive, then you are seen as forgettable. You are expected to be a mix of charisma and accomplishment, energy and elegance, vulnerability and control. You are supposed to be a finished product, but also constantly improving. Confident, but never arrogant. Humble, but never small. It is an exhausting paradox.

People say "be yourself," but what they really mean is "be yourself, as long as that self can bring value." That value is often measured by how useful you are to others, how much status you carry, or how impressive your story sounds. A good personality without credentials is labeled as wasted potential. A quiet thinker is called unambitious. A slow learner is called lazy. And someone without results is often seen as someone without purpose.

The truth is, the world does not reward authenticity by default. It rewards the illusion of authenticity, especially when it is marketable. The most followed people are not necessarily the most insightful. They are the most visible. The loudest voices often drown out the wisest ones. And in the process, people with real character and depth are often overlooked simply because they do not perform loud enough or shine bright enough in a crowded space.

This shift has real consequences. It creates a culture of overcompensation. People start chasing accomplishments not because they feel passionate, but because they are scared of being seen as irrelevant. They curate personalities to match the trends. They force themselves into roles that do not fit, just so they can be accepted, respected, or at least noticed. It is not that they lack identity. It is that they are told their identity alone is not enough.

Think about how this plays out in the workplace. Employers often say they want team players, strong communicators, or people who fit the company culture. But when it comes time to hire, it usually comes down to numbers. Experience, certifications, accolades. People are reduced to bullet points. And if your story does not look impressive on paper, it rarely gets a second glance.

The same thing happens in relationships. People are told to "bring something to the table." But the table itself is rigged. It is not just about who you are anymore, it is about what you offer. And sometimes, who you are gets buried under what you are trying to prove.

Even in education, this mindset creeps in early. Students are graded on performance, ranked against each other, praised for output more than growth. Creativity gets boxed in by rubrics. Compassion is noted but not rewarded. The traits that make someone truly interesting or thoughtful or decent are often seen as side details, not strengths.

So, what happens to people who do not fit into this performance-based model of value? What happens to the quiet ones, the late bloomers, the people who are still figuring it out? What happens to those who have depth, but no platform? What happens to those who are consistent, but not flashy?

They often get overlooked. Or worse, they start believing they have nothing to offer.

That is the paradox.

You grow up being told that character matters. That who you are is more important than what you have. But then you enter the world, and the rules change. You realize charm matters more than kindness. Confidence sells better than integrity. And productivity will almost always get rewarded before emotional intelligence.

None of this means that personality is useless. But it does mean that in this current system, personality is expected to come with proof. It needs to be backed up by visible success, social validation, or economic worth. Otherwise, it is seen as soft, naive, or even irrelevant.

But here is the real truth. What makes a person valuable cannot always be captured by metrics. Some of the best people you will ever meet will not be the ones who are loudest in the room. They will be the ones who show up when no one is watching. The ones who are consistent, kind, honest, even when there is nothing to gain. The world may not always reward that, but that does not make it worthless.

Because value, real value, is not what people say about you when you succeed. It is what remains when you fail. When you lose everything you once used to define yourself. If your value is only tied to what you do, then it will disappear the moment you stop performing. But if your value is tied to who you are, it can endure anything.

You may not be the most impressive, the most followed, or the most decorated. But that does not mean you are not enough. The system may not always see you. But the people who matter will. And if the world ever made you believe your personality is not enough, it is not because you are lacking. It is because the world forgot how to measure people without counting something.

Measured by Output, Defined by Numbers

There is a strange shift that happens sometime after childhood. You are no longer valued just for existing, for laughing or learning or asking questions. You are now judged based on how much you produce, how efficient you are, and how well you meet expectations. You are measured, constantly, by numbers.

Grades. Test scores. Productivity. Income. Net worth.

It does not start with malicious intent. Systems need metrics, and metrics feel like progress. They offer a clean, numerical way to compare people. Who is the best candidate for the job? Who should receive the scholarship? Who deserves more attention or reward? Numbers seem like a fair answer. But fairness is an illusion.

Because behind every number is a person. And behind every person is a story. Numbers erase that. They compress complexity into something digestible and comparable, at the cost of nuance and humanity.

You become your resume. You become your GPA. You become the number on your paycheck. And once that happens, your value feels conditional. If you stop producing, your worth seems to shrink. If your performance dips, you question your identity. You are no longer a human being. You are a human output machine.

This creates a paradox. Society claims to value people, but in practice, it values results. It says everyone matters, but only rewards the ones who can prove it. And the proof has to be in the form of measurable success.

The dangerous part is not just the pressure. It is the internalization. People start believing their worth is equal to their output. If they are not achieving something, they feel like they are wasting time. If they are not winning, they are losing. There is no middle ground. No space to simply be.

This is how burnout begins. You push yourself to meet invisible expectations because slowing down feels like falling behind. You overwork, not out of passion, but out of fear. Fear of becoming irrelevant. Fear of being forgotten. Fear of not being enough.

This is not limited to work. It shows up in relationships too. People begin to think they must earn love, that affection is conditional. They become performers in their own lives, afraid to show weakness, afraid to rest.

It also shows up in the way we view others. We begin to rank people subconsciously, assigning more respect or admiration to those who seem more successful. A person who makes six figures is assumed to be more intelligent or hardworking than someone who does not, even when circumstances and luck play massive roles. A person with a verified social media account is treated as more trustworthy than someone with lived wisdom and no platform.

The world becomes obsessed with metrics. Followers. Likes. Sales. Rankings. Even self-worth gets tied to these metrics. How you feel about yourself can swing wildly based on numbers that fluctuate daily.

What happens to someone who cannot perform? The disabled. The elderly. The unemployed. In a system where output equals value, these people are often overlooked. Their wisdom, empathy, and lived experiences are invisible because they cannot be turned into data points. And so, society marginalizes them, not out of cruelty, but out of a systemic blindness to anything that cannot be monetized or quantified.

You begin to see this everywhere once you notice it. Schools focus more on test scores than learning. Workplaces reward speed over creativity. Politics values polling numbers more than human impact. The deeper truth is buried under spreadsheets and charts.

The paradox is simple but devastating. When you measure a person by output, you lose sight of who they are. And when you define worth by numbers, you reduce a life to statistics. But the soul of a person cannot be graphed. It cannot be scaled or monetized or plotted on a chart. It is not the number of tasks completed. It is how they treat others, how they grow through pain, how they carry themselves through invisible struggles.

Real value is often quiet. It does not always show up in data. Sometimes it looks like listening. Sometimes it looks like rest. Sometimes it looks like saying no. But none of those things show up on a performance review. None of them help you climb a corporate ladder or get accepted into a competitive program.

And yet, they are the things that define us.

The irony is that the most productive people are often the most insecure. They keep producing because they are afraid of what happens if they stop. But a person's worth should not disappear when they step away from work. You do not become worthless just because you are tired.

If we want to create a better world, we have to start redefining value. We have to separate it from performance. A person is not a product. A child is not a future salary. An artist is not only valid when they are popular. A life is not only meaningful when it is efficient.

There are parts of you that cannot be captured in data, and those parts are often the most important. The parts that love, forgive, wonder, and care. The parts that fall apart and put themselves back together. These are the things that numbers cannot measure, and yet, they are the things that matter most.

Who Are You Without a Mirror?

Strip away your name, your achievements, your job title, your income. Remove your social media, your clothing style, your test scores, your reputation. What is left?

This is not a philosophical exercise. It is a question that lives at the heart of how we understand human value. Most people cannot answer it comfortably. Because most people have never had to.

Society hands you a mirror early. You are taught to look into it to understand who you are. But the mirror is not made of glass. It is made of feedback. Likes, comments, compliments, praise, test results, awards, acceptance letters, salary offers. These reflections start to become your identity.

You are not just living. You are being watched, compared, and measured. And eventually, you start adjusting your life to fit the reflection rather than the other way around. You become who others think you are, or who you think they want you to be. The real you begins to dissolve in the performance.

This is the paradox. You are told to "be yourself," while also being given thousands of signals about what that self should look like. The world says authenticity is valuable, but only if it fits into a marketable mold.

As a result, people build versions of themselves to survive. Personas that perform well in certain settings. Some learn to be agreeable to gain approval. Some learn to be aggressive to earn respect. Some become quieter to avoid judgment. Others become louder so they are not forgotten. None of it is fake in the traditional sense. It is an adaptation.

But adaptation becomes wild when it replaces identity. You begin to wonder whether your thoughts are truly yours, or shaped by the need to be accepted. You start asking whether your ambitions are real, or just echoes of what success is supposed to look like. It becomes difficult to tell the difference.

That confusion grows over time. Because no mirror is ever accurate. Every person reflects something different back to you. Your boss sees you one way. Your friends another. Your parents something else entirely. You are split across every relationship you have, performing slightly differently in each.

And the worst part? You cannot escape the mirror. Even solitude is no longer truly private. People curate their alone time, their journals, their personal thoughts, hoping they still align with the identity they are projecting. The pressure never stops.

So who are you, really?

Who are you when no one is watching? Who are you when you stop trying to impress, persuade, entertain, or prove?

That question terrifies people. Because in a world that constantly asks, "What do you do?" Most people have no answer when asked, "Who are you?"

Some chase new identities to avoid the discomfort. Reinventing yourself is seen as noble. And in many ways, it can be. Growth is real. People change. But there is a difference between growth and erasure. Reinventing yourself out of fear is not liberation. It is a new disguise.

You can be praised endlessly and still feel unknown. You can succeed wildly and still feel lost. Because the mirror was never built to show you who you are. It only shows you what others want to see.

That is why people who lose their jobs sometimes fall into crisis. Why retired athletes feel aimless. Why students who graduate suddenly feel empty. When the identity attached to your output disappears, so does the sense of self. And what is left often feels unfamiliar.

This is not just about careers. It is about meaning. The search for self-worth becomes a search for mirrors. We look for validation in relationships, status, platforms, even pain. Some people cling to victimhood because it gives them identity. Others chase conflict because it makes them feel important.

But the only way out of the trap is to stop chasing reflections altogether.

To stop asking, "How do people see me?" and start asking, "What do I believe when no one is listening?" To stop asking, "What should I become?" and start asking, "What have I forgotten?"

Because the real self does not shout. It waits. Beneath all the masks and performances, there is something steady. Something that has not changed, even as everything else has. That part of you may not make money. It may not win awards. It may not look impressive on paper. But it is yours.

The value of a person cannot be seen in a mirror. It cannot be tracked in a spreadsheet or reflected in applause. It is found in how they treat others when there is nothing to gain. It is found in how they respond to silence, not just noise. It is found in their ability to sit with who they are, without needing permission to be that way.

So ask yourself again. Who are you without a mirror?

And if the answer is, "I do not know," that is not a failure. That is where it starts.

The Paradox of Progress

The Faster We Advance, the Emptier We Feel

There has never been a moment in human history where things moved faster than they do today. Information travels at the speed of thought, cities rise in months, and new technology becomes outdated before it can fully integrate. We are told that progress is good, that it is the measure of a successful society. But in that pursuit of speed, something essential is quietly slipping away. We are advancing so quickly that we have stopped asking what it is we are actually advancing toward.

It starts with how we define progress. Most people equate it with convenience, efficiency, and access. The ability to communicate across the globe instantly, to automate tasks that used to take hours, to never run out of entertainment. These are sold to us as victories. But what happens when convenience becomes dependence? When we begin to feel anxious without constant updates, when silence feels like a problem to solve, not a space to think?

The more technology grows, the more we expect life to feel easier. And in many ways, it does. You can order groceries from your bed, start a business from your phone, and learn any skill online in minutes. But this flood of access also brings invisible weight. The pressure to be productive all the time. The fear of falling behind. The illusion that if you are not moving forward, you are failing.

That pressure is not just emotional, it is biological. We are not built for this pace. Our brains evolved in a world of seasons, cycles, and rest. Now, we measure time in unread emails and seconds shaved off loading screens. We are always available, always reachable, always "on." And even though the world has sped up, we have not adapted to it. We are still human, which means we still burn out. We still need time to reflect. We still need slowness. But progress does not wait for permission.

Think about the workplace. Automation and artificial intelligence are replacing tasks faster than humans can learn new ones. A job that used to provide thirty years of stable income now disappears in a decade, maybe less. Skillsets expire. Careers evaporate. People scramble to reinvent themselves, not because they want to grow, but because the system forces them to keep up.

The very tools meant to empower us have created new forms of insecurity. You can now reach millions of people online, yet still feel irrelevant. You can access more data than entire generations before you, yet feel more confused. We have built a world where speed and scale matter more than meaning. Where being first is more important than being right. And where appearing successful has replaced actually feeling fulfilled.

This is not just a problem of technology. It is a problem of mindset. We have convinced ourselves that faster is always better, that growth is always positive, that slowing down is weakness. But progress without direction is just movement. And movement without reflection becomes chaos.

Look at how we consume news. Headlines are designed to grab attention, not to inform. Outrage spreads faster than truth. Every new development feels urgent, even when it is not. The result is that we feel constantly overwhelmed by the world, not because more is happening, but because more is being delivered to us without a filter. Our minds are cluttered. We know a little about everything, and understand nothing deeply.

Social media accelerates this even further. Trends change daily. Algorithms reward reaction, not thought. People chase virality because attention has become currency. But attention is not connection. You can have ten million views and still feel alone. You can post every day and still wonder if anyone actually knows who you are. The speed at which things happen now makes everything feel disposable. Moments are forgotten before they are processed. Stories are old before they are finished.

Even in personal growth, we rush. People want instant results from long term change. They want to meditate for a week and feel healed. They want to read a book and become enlightened. But real growth is slow. It is uncomfortable. It cannot be downloaded. And yet we are trained to chase the next solution, the next hack, the next shortcut. We are running faster and faster toward something we cannot name.

The paradox of progress is that it gives us more power while making us feel more powerless. It expands our choices while increasing our confusion. It removes friction while removing meaning. Every advancement solves a problem, but often creates a new one. And yet we rarely stop to ask what we are losing in the process.

When everything is optimized, what happens to things that are meant to be imperfect? Relationships, for example, are not efficient. They take time, patience, and effort. They require sitting with discomfort. But in a world that celebrates speed, those traits feel out of place. People want connection without vulnerability. They want love without mess. They want belonging without effort. And when it does not happen fast enough, they move on. Swipe left. Unfollow. Start over.

Art suffers the same fate. Music, writing, film, all now compete for attention in an endless scroll. Depth is replaced by volume. Quantity over quality. The pressure to produce quickly drains the soul out of creativity. Artists are expected to become content machines, not thinkers. Ideas are expected to be viral, not meaningful. And in that environment, it becomes harder to make anything that truly lasts.

Progress has its place. It can cure diseases, reduce suffering, expand access. It can lift people out of poverty, connect distant cultures, and protect the planet. But it is only valuable when guided by purpose. When used without thought, it becomes noise. When worshiped without question, it becomes destructive.

The faster we move, the more deliberate we must be. Otherwise, we will find ourselves surrounded by everything we ever wanted, and still feel empty. We will build a world that runs efficiently, but lacks humanity. We will succeed by every external measure, but wonder why we feel lost.

There is nothing wrong with wanting to advance. But we have to ask, at what cost? What are we sacrificing for the sake of speed? What are we leaving behind in our rush forward? And most importantly, is the destination worth the pace?

That is the question this chapter asks. Not whether progress is good or bad, but whether our obsession with speed is causing us to forget what it means to live well. Whether, in trying to improve everything, we are forgetting the things that made life meaningful in the first place.

Innovation Solves Everything, Until It Doesn't

We live in a time where innovation is praised as the highest achievement of modern society. New ideas, new technologies, new systems, all designed to fix problems faster than the last version. Innovation is marketed as a solution to everything, poverty, climate change, social inequality, burnout, even loneliness. If there is a problem, somewhere someone is trying to build an app for it. But as much as innovation has improved the world in measurable ways, it also hides a paradox. It fixes what is broken, while sometimes breaking what once worked.

This is not an argument against innovation. It is an examination of what happens when we blindly assume that all innovation is good, or that faster, newer, and more complex automatically means better. Because when you dig into it, not every problem has a technological solution. Not every issue can be solved by creating another platform or another device. And often, in trying to simplify the world, we make it harder to navigate.

Take healthcare. Medical advancements have extended life expectancy, cured diseases, and reduced infant mortality. But at the same time, modern healthcare systems have become bloated with bureaucracy, cost inflation, and depersonalization. Patients are often seen as data points, not people. Visits become rushed, interactions transactional. Innovation made medicine more powerful, but also more distant. It gave us tools, but removed touch.

Online learning platforms have made knowledge more accessible than ever before. You can learn coding, language, economics, and philosophy from top universities without ever stepping foot in a classroom. But this ease of access has not translated into deeper understanding for most. Students binge videos, skim materials, and jump from topic to topic without mastery. The human structure, mentorship, and shared environment of traditional education, once considered burdensome, is now being missed. Because information is not the same as wisdom. Knowing more does not mean understanding more.

We often forget that some innovations create dependence. Social media, for example, began as a tool to connect people across distances. But it has gradually morphed into a source of addiction, anxiety, and manipulation. Algorithms optimize for attention, not connection. Platforms promote outrage over nuance. And the people building these systems are not evil, they are simply rewarded for engagement, not ethics. The system innovated its way into a trap. It solved the problem of distance, but introduced new problems of distortion.

Innovation is a double-edged sword. Remote work, automation, and artificial intelligence have made companies more efficient. But they have also made workers feel more isolated, expendable, and disconnected. In the name of flexibility, many lost communities. In the name of efficiency, many lost job security. The same tools that empower freelancers to earn from anywhere also expose them to constant competition, unstable income, and lack of benefits. The solution created new vulnerabilities.

What drives this paradox is the assumption that all human problems are systems problems. That if we just optimize the code, redesign the platform, or rework the architecture, the people will adapt and the issue will disappear. But not every challenge is structural. Some are emotional, cultural, or ethical. And when you try to solve those with technology, you often end up making things worse, or at least more confusing.

Look at the way we handle loneliness. Apps offer instant connection, virtual friends, and community forums. But for many, the result is not connection, but the simulation of it. A profile picture is not a friend. A like is not love. A video call is not presence. We have innovated our way out of physical isolation, only to land in emotional isolation. We are surrounded by people, but starved for intimacy.

The problem is not just the tools, it is how we define success. Most innovators are rewarded not for solving meaningful problems, but for creating growth, raising capital, or capturing attention. So they chase scale, even when small would be better. They pursue speed, even when patience is needed. And they simplify metrics, even when the issue is complex.

It is hard to blame them. They are operating within a system that values profit over purpose, and convenience over contemplation. A system that celebrates innovation for its novelty, not its necessity. And once an innovation is introduced, it becomes difficult to reverse. We adapt too quickly. We get used to the convenience. We forget what life was like before.

This is not a call to stop innovating. It is a call to think more deeply about why we innovate, how we define progress, and what we are willing to lose in the name of improvement. Because sometimes the solution to a problem is not a new system, but a return to something old. A deeper conversation. A slower pace. A community that listens. A tradition that grounds us.

We need to stop asking, what can we build next, and start asking, what should we build at all. Not every idea needs to scale. Not every problem needs a product. Not every trend deserves investment. Innovation should be a tool in service of values, not a replacement for them.

In the end, the danger is not in innovation itself. The danger is in forgetting that people are not machines. That culture is not software. That some wounds do not heal faster just because we automate the bandage.

So yes, innovation solves many things. But it also creates blind spots. And if we are not careful, we will keep solving symptoms while ignoring the root. We will keep building tools for connection while forgetting how to connect. We will keep optimizing systems until we remove the very things that made life worth living.

Progress is not just about what we make. It is about who we become. And if we become people who believe every answer can be built in code, we may one day wake up in a world that is perfectly functional, and completely hollow.

The Faster We Move, the Less We Arrive

In a world that moves at the speed of light, slowness has become almost shameful. Fast food, fast delivery, fast communication, fast decisions. We are taught that speed equals success, that urgency is efficiency, that moving quickly means you are winning. There is an unspoken rule that if you are not keeping up, you are falling behind. And so, we rush.

We rush through school, picking majors before we understand ourselves. We rush into jobs, into commitments, into routines that seem acceptable only because they are familiar. We scroll past headlines, skip through videos, and jump to conclusions. The goal is no longer understanding, it is simply to get through things as quickly as possible. More is better, faster is best.

But what if speed is costing us the very things we are rushing toward? That is the paradox. The faster we move, the more progress we expect, but the less fulfilled we feel. We run from task to task, meeting to meeting, achievement to achievement, believing that momentum will bring meaning. But momentum is not direction. Acceleration is not purpose. A life that moves quickly is not always a life that goes somewhere.

Take career development as an example. Many young people now feel an invisible timer running above their heads. They think if they do not land the right internship by age twenty, get promoted by twenty five, and reach financial independence by thirty, they have failed. They treat their lives like startup timelines, forgetting that even companies pivot, restart, and sometimes collapse. And when things do not happen fast, they question their worth instead of questioning the timeline.

It is not just careers. Relationships are affected too. People swipe, text, match, meet, and date in the span of days. There is little space for depth. There is no pause to understand someone's complexity. If things are not instantly perfect, they are discarded. The expectation is immediate compatibility, instant chemistry, and zero conflict. But real relationships are not born in speed. They grow in patience, in silence, in repetition. Slowness does not mean failure. It often means care.

The obsession with speed extends to how we learn, how we heal, and how we grow. There are shortcuts promised everywhere. Learn a language in thirty days. Heal from trauma with a five step course. Become a millionaire by next year. The idea is that any delay is a defect, any pause is a problem. But some things cannot be rushed. Wisdom requires reflection. Trust requires time. Real confidence is not downloaded, it is built, slowly, from experience.

And yet, this culture of urgency forces us into quantity over quality. We believe doing more is always better, that completing ten tasks halfway is more impressive than doing two things with full attention. But that mindset is flawed. Because sometimes, less is more. Sometimes, slower is better. Sometimes, quality over quantity is not just a nice phrase, it is a principle for living. A single meaningful moment carries more value than a dozen that are forgettable.

Technology convinces us that everything should be instant because it can be. But humans do not operate like servers. We have emotions, fatigue, doubt, and memories that take time to process. When everything around us speeds up, we start blaming ourselves for being slow, when in reality, we are moving at a human pace in a machine world.

This misalignment between natural rhythm and external velocity creates internal conflict. People feel anxious without knowing why. They feel behind, even if there is no race. They feel overwhelmed, even if nothing is visibly wrong. That is what happens when life moves faster than your mind can process. You become a passenger in your own story, unable to catch up with the events you are living.

It also makes decisions harder. When things move quickly, you feel pressure to act immediately. You say yes before thinking. You commit before you are ready. You respond to things you have not fully felt. And in doing so, you risk building a life based on speed, not alignment. You may achieve what you aimed for, only to realize it is not what you wanted.

One of the cruelest aspects of this paradox is that fast paced living is often mistaken for ambition. People who move nonstop, who schedule every hour, who never rest, they are praised. They are seen as disciplined, hungry, driven. But constant motion is not always noble. Sometimes, it is avoidance. Sometimes, fear is disguised as productivity. It is the fear of stillness, because stillness might force us to face questions we are not ready to answer.

And so we stay moving. We consume content without absorbing it. We multitask until nothing gets our full attention. We chase progress until we forget the point of arrival. We say we are building a better future, but we sacrifice the present in the process.

We live in a time where slowness is treated like failure, when in truth, slowness is often the birthplace of wisdom. It is in the pause that we notice what matters. It is in the wait that we realize what is worth pursuing. Speed has its place, but so does stillness. Movement is necessary, but so is direction.

If you spend your life running without asking why, you may one day reach the end and realize you never actually lived. You moved, but you did not arrive. You achieved, but you did not feel. You grew, but you did not know what for.

The answer is not to stop moving altogether. The answer is to reclaim the right to move at your own pace. To understand that your timeline does not have to match anyone else's. That slowness is not laziness, and silence is not emptiness. Sometimes, the most powerful progress is invisible, the kind that happens inside you when you stop long enough to hear your own thoughts.

It is time we stop measuring life by speed and start measuring it by depth. A slow moment that changes you is more valuable than a fast year you cannot remember. A single decision made with clarity is more powerful than a dozen made under pressure. A life lived with attention, even if quiet, will always be more meaningful than one rushed through at full volume.

Progress is not a race. It is a journey. And if you want to actually arrive, you have to be willing to slow down.

Success That Feels Wrong

Some people achieve everything they aimed for, yet feel hollow once they get there. They win awards, earn promotions, build reputations, but when they sit alone with their thoughts, something feels off. There is a reason why some of the most publicly admired individuals feel privately lost. The truth is, just because the world claps for you, does not mean you are on the right stage.

Success is often measured by how it looks, not how it feels. We are taught to aim for external milestones. Get the degree. Land the job. Grow your income. Build the brand. These markers are easy to track and easy to praise. But they are not always aligned with who we are. Sometimes we pursue them just because they are there, because someone told us they mattered. Not because they actually do.

This creates a painful paradox. The more you chase what others reward, the more you risk losing your connection with yourself. You begin to silence the parts of you that do not fit the path you are on. Maybe you are an artist at heart but you are stuck in finance. Maybe you care deeply about people but work in a system that treats them like numbers. At first, you try to ignore it. But the dissonance grows. It shows up as burnout, fatigue, quiet frustration.

Eventually, you are left asking a question no one prepared you for. What if I am succeeding at the wrong thing?

It is a terrifying thought, because success is supposed to bring relief. It is supposed to mean you made it. But for many, it just raises more questions. If I feel unfulfilled now, after all I have done, what was the point of doing it? Why did I sacrifice so much to be here, if I still feel incomplete?

This is where many people find themselves stuck. They feel guilty for not being satisfied. After all, others would kill to have their opportunities. So they keep going, pretending the discomfort is temporary. They try to convince themselves that more achievement will fix it. But deep down, they know the real issue is not quantity. It is quality.

This is where the phrase "quality over quantity" becomes more than just a cliché. It is not about having fewer things. It is about having the right things. The right goals. The right reasons. The right pace. A slow life aligned with your core values will always feel better than a fast life that contradicts them. But that kind of wisdom is not easy to access when the world rewards speed, productivity, and performance.

There is also the issue of identity. When success becomes your identity, failure becomes a threat to your existence. You start to feel like you cannot stop or slow down, even when you want to. You have spent so long climbing the ladder that you forgot to ask if it is leaning against the right wall. And when it is not, turning around feels impossible.

So what do you do when your success feels wrong?

You pause. You reflect. You look inward instead of outward. You ask uncomfortable but necessary questions. What did I used to care about before the world told me what to want? What parts of myself have I ignored in the name of achievement? Who am I when I am not performing for praise?

The answers are not easy. Sometimes, they require change. Not just minor adjustments, but real shifts in direction. And that is scary. It might mean disappointing people. It might mean starting over. It might mean losing temporary approval to gain long-term peace.

But what is the cost of ignoring it?

The longer you stay misaligned, the heavier it gets. The more your days feel like performance rather than purpose. And eventually, even the praise stops working. It no longer fills the emptiness it used to distract you from.

Real success is not about reaching a finish line. It is about feeling right in your own skin while you move through life. It is about alignment, not applause. It is about building something that reflects who you really are, not who you are trying to impress.

So, if you ever get to the top and still feel lost, do not see it as failure. See it as a signal. A chance to rewrite your definition of success before it is too late.

The Paradox Of Originality

The Desire to Be Different

Originality has always been romanticized, not just as a creative virtue but as a personal one. People admire those who stand out, who do not blend in, who seem to operate by their own rules. But beneath that admiration is a quiet tension. How does one become different in a world that rewards sameness?

There is a hidden economy of originality. It is not just about having an idea. It is about having it first. Or presenting it better. Or branding it in a way that makes it hard to replicate. The problem is, most things that appear original are not. They are modifications, combinations, or reintroductions of old frameworks with updated language.

Yet the pursuit of being different continues. People are not just trying to build careers or reputations. They are trying to build identities that feel uncommon. Not because difference always leads to truth, but because being different implies worth. If everyone else is doing something and you are not, then maybe you know something they do not. Maybe your distance from the crowd is proof that you are ahead.

This logic can be dangerous. Sometimes it leads to growth, experimentation, and new understanding. Other times, it leads to isolation and a rejection of anything mainstream, not because it is wrong, but simply because it is popular. Originality becomes rebellion for its own sake, disconnected from value.

You see it in art, business, and culture. A product that works too well is called unoriginal. A message that resonates with too many people is dismissed as surface level. A person who appeals to both sides of an argument is considered inauthentic. As if originality must always be controversial, misunderstood, or lonely.

But real originality is often quiet. It does not demand recognition. It does not exist to provoke or impress. It is the result of depth, not noise. It is shaped over time, not rushed to market.

That is where the paradox emerges. The louder the world gets, the harder it becomes to know if your voice is your own. The pressure to stand out can be just as limiting as the pressure to fit in. You might think you are being original, but you are just following a different pattern, one designed to look independent while feeding the same need for approval.

The desire to be different starts to resemble a competition. Everyone is trying to be unique, yet operating within the same environment, using the same tools, chasing the same kind of validation. It becomes exhausting, not because people are failing, but because the definition of originality itself has been corrupted.

What if being original has less to do with how you are seen and more to do with how you think? Not the opinions you post, but the questions you ask. Not the roles you play, but the assumptions you refuse to carry. What if originality is not a performance, but a perspective?

That kind of originality does not always show on the surface. It cannot be captured in a picture or condensed into a bio. It is not easy to monetize. And that is why it is so rare. Because the world does not reward quiet clarity. It rewards packaging.

But you do not need to be a spectacle to be original. You need to be honest. Not brutally honest in the way that demands attention, but consistently honest in the way that reshapes your decisions. You need to be brave enough to think deeply even when no one notices. To form opinions slowly. To resist the rush of jumping on every trend. To stay curious longer than most people are willing to.

True originality is not about looking different. It is about thinking clearly when most people are confused. It is about caring more about truth than applause. It is not loud, but it is firm. It is not popular, but it is grounded. And it often comes with the price of being misunderstood.

That is the myth. People think originality means being recognized. But often, it means going unnoticed. You are not optimizing for views or building a highlight reel. You are not trying to be different. You just are.

The Identity Copy Loop

Originality is not only marketed through what you buy or create. It is now sold as a personality. As if there is a pure version of you that exists, untouched by influence, waiting to be discovered. But what if that version never existed?

Who you think you are has been shaped by everything around you. And that is not a weakness, it is a fact. Your personality is not a blueprint you created. It is a collection of copied instincts, repeated phrases, mirrored habits, and trial and error built from every interaction you have ever had. You copy others without realizing it, and they copy you back. This is not theft. This is how humans learn.

We copy to survive. Children mirror their parents before they understand what words mean. Teenagers copy their friends so they are not left out. Adults copy social cues to succeed in professional spaces. And the internet, especially now, has turned imitation into culture.

Social media is the loudest proof. A few trends explode across the platform, and suddenly, millions are posting the same jokes, outfits, voiceovers, or reactions. Everyone is trying to be seen, yet everyone looks exactly the same. We think we are building identity. What we are really doing is participating in a loop of curated replication.

Even rebellion is recycled. You post an opinion no one asked for. You think you are breaking the mold. But scroll far enough, and you will find thousands of others who did it first. Even uniqueness has a template.

And here lies the paradox. The more you try to stand out, the more you become a product of what already exists. The louder you scream for individuality, the more you become dependent on the audience you are performing for. If your identity needs to be noticed to feel real, is it actually yours?

The desire to be original often becomes a trap. Not because people are fake, but because the system rewards familiarity dressed up as difference. Companies do not want real originality, they want profitable variations. Clothing brands want you to "express yourself," as long as it fits within seasonal trends. Music labels want fresh sounds that still feel like last summer's hits. Schools encourage "thinking outside the box," as long as you use the right rubric.

So, you are told to express yourself while being graded for fitting in. You are told to be unique while being fed the same content as everyone else. You are asked to show your voice, but only if that voice fits the structure that came before.

What makes this worse is how people now monetize their identity. Your look, your tone, your personal story, all of it can be marketed. And while that seems empowering, it turns people into brands. You are no longer just yourself, you are your follower count, your bio, your aesthetic, your algorithm. Even your vulnerability becomes performance. It becomes hard to tell where your actual self ends and where the marketed version begins.

And still, we crave to be seen as different. Because being different signals value. In a competitive world, originality is power. So we try to construct uniqueness like a résumé. We search for hobbies no one else has, opinions that spark engagement, or aesthetics that look effortless and exclusive. We shape our identity through strategic contrast, defining ourselves by what we are not, rather than what we actually are.

But if all of that is just another reflection of the environment, if it is still built on copying and modifying, then what does it really mean to be yourself?

Maybe the answer is not to stop copying. Because copying is human. Copying is learning. Maybe the answer is to be more conscious of what you choose to keep. Instead of chasing an identity that looks original, focus on one that feels honest.

Ask yourself, who am I when no one is watching? What would I wear, say, or create if it was never going to be posted, liked, or judged?

That is when something real starts to form. Not original in the sense that it came from nothing. But original in the sense that you chose it. You understood the influence. You saw the loop. And you still picked what meant something to you.

That is how identity becomes yours, not when it is never touched by the world, but when you finally take ownership of the parts that do.

The Echo Chamber of Creativity

There is a strange irony in how creativity spreads. The more something resonates, the more it gets copied. The very act of creating something that moves people increases the chances that it will be diluted. A powerful idea does not stay singular for long. It becomes a format, a strategy, a model for others to follow.

And in that process, something gets lost.

We are living in an age where originality is praised, but replication is rewarded. The algorithm does not promote the most thoughtful content. It promotes what has worked before. What is safe. What is familiar. The result is a cycle where creators, thinkers, and innovators are pressured to repeat what already exists, just slightly modified.

It creates an echo chamber. A space where voices sound different on the surface, but all come from the same source. Slight variations of the same insights. Recycled opinions dressed in new language. And it is hard to notice because it feels fresh at first. It feels new because it is new to you. But once you zoom out, you begin to see patterns.

Books start to read the same. Advice starts to blend together. Art loses its edge. It all becomes safe.

That is the tragedy of creative echo chambers. They do not kill creativity instantly. They slowly bleed it out. They make it easy to produce and hard to risk. They encourage the creator to think less about discovery and more about performance. About what will sell, what will trend, what will get you invited to the table.

And it is not just in art or writing. You see it in business, politics, fashion, and thought leadership. The same quotes, the same posturing, the same packaging. It is not that people lack talent. It is that the environment rewards predictability.

You might think you are creating something meaningful. And maybe you are. But if the entire creative process is shaped by fear, fear of failure, fear of being misunderstood, fear of being overlooked, then the final product is shaped by that fear too. It becomes a shadow of what it could have been.

Originality begins to look risky. Not because it is bad, but because it might not perform.

So people stop experimenting. They stop taking chances. They stop following the uncomfortable idea and instead follow the proven one. The safe route. The path of least resistance.

And here comes the paradox: the more crowded the creative space becomes, the harder it is to be original, and the more desperately people want to appear original. So they dress up recycled thoughts in louder branding. They overstate weak points. They try harder to be seen, not heard. Because attention has replaced authenticity as the metric for success.

But true creativity does not emerge from noise. It emerges from stillness. It comes from people who are willing to pause, to think, to question their influences instead of imitating them. People who do not just want to say something new, but want to understand something fully.

To do that requires a level of detachment. You have to step away from the feed, from the likes, from the external metrics. You have to care more about what you are creating than how it will be received. That sounds noble, but it is brutal in practice. Especially when your income, identity, or career depends on being heard.

It is easier to follow a trend than to think from scratch. It is easier to adapt a structure than to invent one. It is easier to echo than to originate.

That is why originality is so rare. Not because people are lazy, but because they are overwhelmed. The pressure to produce fast, to stay relevant, to grow your audience, forces people into patterns that feel creative but are not. They are efficient, not expressive. And that difference matters.

The question is not whether you can be original. The question is whether you can endure the silence that usually comes with being original.

Because real originality does not always get applause. Sometimes it gets ignored. Sometimes it gets rejected. Sometimes it just gets misunderstood.

But if you are creating because it is the only honest thing you can do, then none of that matters. The work is worth doing even if it does not win. That is the quiet defiance of originality in a world full of echoes. It is not about being louder. It is about being real.

Inspiration or Inheritance?

Every generation thinks it is creating something new. That it is pushing boundaries, defying norms, and carving its own path. But when you look closely, the things we celebrate as innovative are often just borrowed ideas, reshaped in modern form. The words are different, the packaging more refined, but the essence is inherited.

And that brings up a deeper question. Where does inspiration end and imitation begin?

We all build on what came before us. Every artist learned by watching others. Every thinker read the thoughts of those who lived before them. Every entrepreneur copied someone else's business model before trying to improve it. None of us start with a blank page, no matter how badly we want to believe we do.

We inherit values, aesthetics, rules, and assumptions. We grow up absorbing what society rewards. We notice who gets applause and who gets ignored. That becomes our reference point. So when we begin to create or speak or act, we are often tracing patterns we did not realize we internalized.

And yet, we want so badly to be seen as original. We want to believe our ideas are untouched, our style is personal, our work is unmistakably ours. But maybe originality is not about being the first to say something. Maybe it is about saying something in a way that only you could, even if the topic has been explored a thousand times.

That is where the difference lies. You can inherit a tradition and still make it your own. You can be influenced without becoming a clone. You can be inspired without losing your voice. But it requires self-awareness. It requires knowing when you are borrowing and when you are hiding behind borrowed things.

Because copying is not always obvious. Sometimes it looks like ambition. Sometimes it looks like praise. But if you are repeating a thought just to be accepted, or mimicking a style because it works, then you are not really creating. You are recycling. And recycling can only go so far before it becomes invisible.

The paradox is this, the more you imitate what works, the more forgettable your work becomes. It might succeed in the short term.

It might go viral, sell fast, or win awards. But over time, it disappears into the noise. Because it never truly belonged to you. It never had your fingerprint.

This is not an argument against influence. Influence is inevitable. The question is whether you are curating your influences or being swallowed by them.

That distinction is everything.

When you are intentional, you know what you are borrowing. You know why a certain idea speaks to you, why a specific approach resonates. You understand the history behind it and you choose to carry it forward with care.

But when you are passive, you just absorb. You mimic without knowing. You repeat because it feels familiar. And eventually, you forget what your voice even sounds like.

This is happening more and more. In an era where every creative process is visible, where you can watch behind-the-scenes breakdowns of everything from writing to design to marketing, it is easier than ever to copy without realizing it. We confuse consumption with understanding. We think watching someone build a masterpiece teaches us how to do the same. But watching is not the same as building.

And this flood of access makes us restless. We want to make something great, fast. We want results before identity. We want recognition before discovery. So we jump ahead. We copy what we think is working. And in doing so, we skip the slow, often painful process of figuring out what actually matters to us.

That process is not glamorous. It is not always productive. But it is the only way to create something that lasts.

So what does it mean to be original in a world shaped by inheritance?

It means looking inward before you look outward. It means asking why something speaks to you before you decide to repeat it. It means being honest when you are following someone else's voice instead of your own. And it means being willing to spend time with your thoughts, even when they feel unclear.

Because real originality comes from that space. The space where you are not trying to impress, not trying to perform, but simply trying to understand.

It is slow, difficult, and uncertain. But it is also the only way to leave behind something real.

The Freedom in Limitation

The Prison of Too Much Freedom

We tend to think of freedom as the ultimate prize, the ability to choose, to move, to think, and to speak without restraint. But buried beneath the surface of this noble ideal is a strange and uncomfortable paradox. The more freedom we have, the more lost we sometimes become. When every door is open, the simple act of walking through one feels paralyzing.

Modern society is obsessed with options. You are not just encouraged to make choices, you are overwhelmed by them. There are hundreds of toothpaste brands, dozens of social media platforms, and thousands of career paths. Your devices are personalized. Your advertisements are targeted. Your identity can be constructed, changed, and rebranded as often as you wish. You can be anyone, do anything, live anywhere, and believe whatever you want. At first glance, this seems like progress. But deep down, too many people feel anxious, unfocused, and disconnected.

This is the paradox of choice. Freedom, when stretched too far, becomes a kind of burden. When choice becomes endless, it stops being empowering and starts becoming exhausting.

Imagine walking into a massive room filled with thousands of doors. Behind each one is a different life. One leads to a future in medicine. Another to a life in art. One door hides a family in a quiet town. Another, a career in a fast-paced city. None of the doors are labeled. There is no map. No guide. And you can only open one.

For a while, you stand there imagining what each door could lead to. You tell yourself you are being careful. But really, you are afraid. What if the door you pick is the wrong one? What if the life behind it disappoints you? What if one of the other doors held a better version of your future?

This is not just imagination. This is how many people live, trapped not by limits, but by abundance.

Freedom is often celebrated as the removal of limits. But too often, it simply replaces clear structure with endless uncertainty. In the past, people lived with fewer choices, but clearer expectations. You were born into a trade, a culture, or a belief system. These could be restrictive, even unfair. But they also provided identity and direction. You knew who you were because the world around you made it clear.

Today, the opposite is true. You must decide who you are. You must determine your own beliefs, values, and priorities. You must figure out what success looks like, what truth means, and what happiness really is. That is a heavy responsibility, especially in a world that throws a thousand contradictory messages at you every day.

This pressure creates a quiet form of paralysis. People delay major decisions. They bounce between paths. They keep doors open for as long as possible, terrified that commitment will lead to regret. But what they do not realize is that refusing to choose is also a choice. It is just one that keeps them stuck.

To say yes to one thing is to say no to a hundred others. That is the cost of action. That is the cost of movement. And many would rather avoid that cost than face the fear of being wrong.

In relationships, this shows up as the fear of settling. In careers, it appears as job-hopping, endless side projects, or waiting for the perfect passion. In personal growth, it looks like trying everything but going nowhere. People call it exploring. But often, it is simply avoiding the responsibility of choosing.

This avoidance is not laziness. It is fear. The fear that once you choose, you lose. But what if the real loss is never choosing at all?

There is another angle to this paradox, the illusion of potential. When every path is still available, your future is unlimited. You could become anything. You could do something great. You could build something lasting. But that potential only exists as long as you remain uncommitted. Because once you act, potential becomes reality. And reality will always be more specific, more flawed, and more complicated.

Many people cling to the dream of potential because it feels good. It allows them to believe they are special without having to prove it. But untested potential is just fantasy. And fantasies do not grow. They just repeat until you get tired of them.

Real growth requires focus. And focus requires limits. When you narrow your attention, you sharpen your results. When you cut distractions, you create space for depth. Boundaries bring momentum. A musician improves by staying within the structure of notes. A writer finds their voice through the discipline of language. A scientist progresses by limiting variables. Constraints are not the enemy. They are the source of progress.

In the professional world, many of the most productive people are not those with the most freedom, but those with the strongest boundaries. They work within routines. They protect their time. They say no with confidence. Their days have structure, and their structure allows them to move fast and go deep.

The same truth applies to emotions. People who define their values clearly tend to feel more stable. They are not swayed by every opinion or trend. They know who they are and what they believe. Their inner world is protected by a set of chosen limits.

Limits, when chosen, are not walls. They are blueprints. They are tools. They are acts of self-respect.

But in modern life, this is hard to see. The culture rewards expansion. It tells you to do more, earn more, post more, and consume more. It rewards the illusion of having it all. But people stretched too wide often feel shallow. Their work is inconsistent. Their relationships are fragile. Their goals shift weekly. Their lives move fast, but they do not go anywhere.

Real fulfillment does not come from more. It comes from depth. And depth requires narrowing. You cannot master anything while chasing everything. You cannot connect deeply with others while spreading yourself across a hundred conversations. You cannot build something meaningful without deciding what is actually worth your time.

There is also a social consequence to unlimited freedom. When identity is always changing, connection weakens. When roles are undefined, responsibility dissolves. Trust is harder to build in a world where everyone is constantly reinventing themselves.

And strangely, unlimited freedom can create more conformity. When there is no structure, people imitate each other. They cling to trends. They echo opinions. They chase visibility instead of authenticity.

To escape this trap, you must shift your thinking. The goal is not to do everything. It is to do something that matters. The point is not to collect options, but to pursue something worth committing to.

Freedom is not the absence of limits. It is the power to choose your limits with intention.

Because the real prison is not being forced into one path. The real prison is never taking a step forward because you are scared of closing a door.

And in the end, your potential is only useful if you act on it.

Let others chase everything. Let them stay lost in the room of endless doors.

You, on the other hand, can choose.

And that choice, real, grounded, focused, is what freedom was meant to be.

Why Constraints Spark Creativity

Creativity is often romanticized as boundless freedom — paint splattered on a canvas without rules, words written without structure, music improvised without restriction. We imagine the most creative people as rebels who ignore boundaries, who break rules, who reject limitations. But in truth, creativity does not thrive in chaos. It thrives in structure. It grows not in the absence of boundaries, but because of them.

It is a strange truth that contradicts what many believe. But the paradox is this: creativity is not about having endless options. It is about doing something remarkable with limited ones.

Constraints do not crush creativity. They shape it.

Think about poetry. A haiku must follow a strict pattern of syllables, and yet within that structure, writers produce poems filled with emotion, image, and clarity. The form forces precision. It demands intention. Without the limit, the art would not exist.

Or think of film directors who make low budget movies. Some of the most compelling films in history were not born from endless money or resources, but from having to work around what was missing. The filmmaker who cannot afford elaborate special effects must tell a better story. The director who cannot shoot in dozens of locations must make every frame count. In doing so, they often create something more focused, more human, more lasting.

The same is true in music. Jazz musicians improvise within scales. Classical composers write within keys and time signatures. Songwriters work within rhyme schemes. None of these limits prevent beauty. They make the beauty possible. They give form to what would otherwise be noise.

This is not just about art. It is about how the mind works. The brain, when faced with endless choice, can become overwhelmed. But when given a few key pieces, it begins to build. It fills gaps. It connects dots. It begins to play.

Creativity is not just about expression. It is about problem solving. It is the act of making meaning out of limitations.

This explains why people often become more creative when they are under pressure. A deadline forces a decision. A budget forces efficiency. A missing tool forces innovation. These are not obstacles. They are invitations. The mind responds to them with ingenuity.

In the workplace, some of the most successful startups began not with large teams and generous funding, but with tiny teams trying to solve a real problem using what they had. The limit on resources pushed them to simplify. The lack of experience led them to experiment. The absence of approval allowed them to take risks others would not.

This kind of innovation is not flashy. It is not always glamorous. But it is honest. It comes from people who are not waiting for permission. They are using the tools at their disposal to make something better.

Children are perhaps the best example. Give a child a cardboard box, and they will turn it into a spaceship, a fort, or a race car. Their creativity is not stifled by the simplicity of the material. It is awakened by it. With fewer distractions, their minds are free to invent.

Adults often lose this ability. When faced with a problem, they look for more, more time, more tools, more guidance. But more is not always the answer. Often, it is less that brings the breakthrough.

Consider the field of science. Some of the most important discoveries began with simple questions and simple tools. The microscope revealed a world no one had seen before. The telescope opened the skies. And the people behind these tools worked within strict limits of knowledge, funding, and technology. Still, they pushed forward.

There is something powerful in knowing what you do not have. It forces you to sharpen what you do.

Even in personal development, limitations create growth. A person who struggles with speaking may become an excellent writer. A person who grows up without wealth may develop a sharp sense of resourcefulness. A person who faces rejection may build deeper empathy. These are not weaknesses. They are starting points.

Constraints force us to answer hard questions. What do I really want to say? What matters most? What am I willing to work around or fight through? The answers to these questions give direction.

Without limits, you can drift. But with them, you find purpose.

Many people avoid constraints because they feel uncomfortable. They feel like failure. But discomfort is where creativity lives. It is where ideas are tested, refined, and reshaped.

There is also humility in working within limits. It reminds you that you are not above the world you live in. You must adapt to it. You must listen to it. You must respond, not just impose.

That humility makes the work better. It makes the artist more honest. It makes the thinker more thoughtful. It makes the creator more connected to the people they serve.

The modern world often sells the idea that freedom is the ability to do anything at any time. But people who live like that often feel scattered and unfulfilled. They chase novelty instead of depth. They seek quantity over quality. And in doing so, they rarely finish what they start.

True creativity is not fast. It is not always fun. It is the long process of making something meaningful within the limits you are given.

And sometimes, those limits are self-imposed. A person who chooses to write a book in thirty days is giving themselves a creative limit. An artist who paints only in black and white is choosing a constraint. A team that decides to build a product using only recycled materials is setting a rule that will challenge them. These limits are not weaknesses. They are declarations.

They say, this is the space I will work in. And within this space, I will do something excellent.

The most creative people in the world are not those with endless resources. They are those who know how to focus. Who understand that energy is finite. That attention is precious. That clarity matters more than noise.

Creativity needs space, yes. But not too much space. It needs boundaries. It needs edges. It needs a shape to push against.

Because that tension, that pressure, that dance between what is and what could be, that is where the real magic happens.

Saying No as a Form of Power

Most people are taught that power means saying yes. Say yes to opportunity. Say yes to experience. Say yes to growth. But the paradox is, the most powerful people are not those who say yes to everything. They are the ones who know when and how to say no.

Saying no is not a weakness. It is control. It is focus. It is the ability to protect your time, your mind, and your energy. When you say no, you are making a statement about what matters. You are refusing to be pulled in a hundred directions. You are deciding to move with purpose.

There is a fear built into "no". We think that saying no will disappoint others. That it will close doors. That it will make us look selfish or ungrateful. But that fear often leads to exhaustion. People who cannot say no end up overwhelmed. They commit to too much. They agree to things that are misaligned with their values. And slowly, they lose themselves.

Saying yes to everything does not mean you are strong. It often means you are afraid to disappoint. Or worse, you do not know what you want.

Real strength is selective. It is measured. It does not chase every chance. It builds around what matters most.

In relationships, saying no sets boundaries. It teaches others how to treat you. If you say yes to every demand, every favor, every last-minute call, you send the message that your needs do not matter. That your time is available to be taken. But when you begin to say no, kindly and clearly, people learn to respect you. And if they do not, they were never truly respecting you in the first place.

In work, saying no is strategic. You cannot take on every project. You cannot be in every meeting. You cannot accept every job offer. There is always more to do. But more does not always mean better. When you say no to the wrong things, you make space for the right ones. You give your best effort to fewer tasks, and the quality increases. Your focus sharpens. Your impact grows.

There is also power in saying no to yourself.

No, I will not check my phone again.

No, I will not say yes out of guilt.

No, I will not keep chasing something that drains me.

Discipline is not only about what you choose to do. It is also about what you deliberately avoid. And that kind of discipline builds integrity. You begin to trust yourself. You begin to make promises you can actually keep.

Many people think freedom is about having more choices. But real freedom often comes from the opposite. It comes from limits you choose. From commitments you honor. From distractions you eliminate.

This is especially true in the digital world. Social media, news, constant notifications, they beg for your attention. And every yes to them is a no to something else. A no to quiet. A no to deep thought. A no to real connection.

When you say no to noise, you reclaim your mind.

And yet, saying no is uncomfortable. It goes against the social training many people have received. We are raised to be agreeable, to go along, to avoid conflict. But constant agreement is not kindness. It is avoidance. Real kindness includes honesty. Real respect includes boundaries.

Some people will be surprised when you begin to say no. Especially if you have built a pattern of always saying yes. They might question you. Push back. Try to guilt you. That is part of the shift. But over time, your no becomes clearer. Firmer. Healthier. And the right people will stay. The wrong ones will fall away.

Saying no does not make you difficult. It makes you intentional.

Think of it like architecture. A strong building is not built by piling bricks at random. It is built by design. Every line, every space, every limit serves a purpose. Your life is no different. You are not just collecting experiences. You are shaping something. And saying no is one of the tools that gives it form.

Even in creative work, saying no matters. You say no to distractions so you can write. You say no to perfection so you can finish. You say no to external pressure so you can make something honest. These refusals are not lazy. They are sacred. They are how the work gets done.

And in ambition, saying no is how you find clarity. There will always be new goals, new ideas, new temptations. But if you chase them all, you achieve none. The people who build meaningful things in the world are not scattered. They are focused. They know what they are not doing. They make peace with that.

One of the most powerful questions you can ask is, what am I willing to miss?

Because you cannot have everything. That is not defeat. That is design. The act of choosing is also the act of refusing. And the more thoughtful your refusals, the more powerful your life becomes.

There is a dignity in a clear no. It means you are awake. It means you are paying attention. It means you value your time and your life.

It is easy to drift. To say yes without thinking. To agree because it is easier. But drifting never leads to depth. Drift leads to regret.

So when you say no, say it with confidence. Say it without apology. Say it because you know what your yes is worth.

You Can Do Anything, So You Do Nothing

There is a strange weight that comes with freedom. The kind of freedom that tells you the world is open, the paths are infinite, and the only thing stopping you is yourself. On the surface, it sounds like empowerment. But deep down, it can feel like quiet chaos.

In past generations, choices were limited. You would often take over the family business, follow the same trade as your parents, or settle into a path that was clear, expected, and largely unquestioned. Today, we are told we can do anything. That freedom is a gift. That not having a plan means you are simply waiting for the right one to appear. But what if too much freedom is not freedom at all? What if it is a trap dressed up as a possibility?

When you can be anything, how do you decide? If the answer is everything, it makes choosing one thing feel like a loss. Every door you walk through means shutting another. Every commitment feels like betrayal to another dream you could have chased. You sit with open tabs in your brain, half-formed plans and abandoned goals. You daydream about one life while trying to live another.

This is not laziness. This is paralysis. The kind that comes from drowning in options. You wake up in the morning with a dozen things you could do. Write a book. Start a business. Apply for a scholarship. Learn a language. Train for a marathon. Then the day ends, and you have done none of them. Not because you do not care. But because you care too much, and the weight of doing it wrong keeps you from starting.

It is not that you are not motivated. It is that you are overwhelmed. Every option feels loaded with consequence. Pick the wrong major, and you are "stuck" in the wrong career. Choose the wrong job, and you fall behind. Choose the wrong partner, and you waste years. The fear of wasting time becomes the reason you waste time.

This is the paradox of potential. When everything is possible, nothing feels concrete. You live in a loop of maybe, always almost, never fully committed. You avoid the discomfort of choosing by pretending you are just waiting for clarity. But clarity often comes after action, not before it. You learn by doing. But doing requires risking being wrong, and many people are terrified of that.

We also romanticize success stories. We admire the ones who knew what they wanted at age twelve and followed through. The prodigies. The focused. The driven. We rarely talk about the ones who changed paths, started late, or figured it out through trial and error. As a result, people feel behind. They feel like if they have not found their one true calling yet, they are failing.

But what if some people are not meant to have one calling? What if life is not about finding a single path, but about making peace with the detours?

The internet has made this worse. Every scroll brings a new idea. A new lifestyle. A new version of success. One moment you want to live in the city and work in finance. The next you want to be a minimalist artist in the woods. Then you see someone traveling the world and feel like that is the answer. The noise is endless, and the comparison is exhausting.

The problem is not the abundance of opportunities. The problem is our inability to filter them. To say no without guilt. To commit without fearing we are missing out. We are addicted to options. And like any addiction, it keeps us from being fully present with what we have.

You look around and see people who seem to have it all figured out. They are building companies, publishing books, and learning new skills. And instead of asking how they do it, you assume they have something you do not. More confidence. More discipline. More talent. But most of the time, the difference is simple. They started. They chose something and gave it enough time to become real.

You can wait your whole life for the perfect idea. Or you can start with a flawed one and grow. Waiting feels safe. But it is also empty. Starting is scary. But it leads somewhere.

The hardest part of any project is not the middle. It is the beginning. The part where you go from nothing to something. From intention to action. That is the bridge most people never cross. They stand on one side imagining, planning, doubting. They tell themselves they need more time. More research. More signs. But deep down, they are just afraid. Because starting means confronting the possibility of failure. Of not being good enough. Of realizing you are not the exception.

But what if failure is part of the path? What if doing something badly is still better than doing nothing at all?

You do not become confident by waiting. You become confident by acting. By proving to yourself that you can handle discomfort. That you can start something and finish it. That you can look uncertainty in the face and move anyway.

It is not always about finding your passion. Sometimes it is about building it. Shaping it. Creating it through repetition and attention. Passion is not a lightning bolt. It is a slow burn. And it needs fuel. Action is the fuel.

When you delay, when you float in indecision, the world does not pause for you. Time moves. Opportunities shift. Other people build. You are not stuck because you lack ability. You are stuck because you refuse to choose.

Choosing is terrifying. But it is also liberating. It gives shape to your time, direction to your energy. It creates boundaries that focus your effort. It gives you something to improve, something to refine, something to fight for.

Doing anything meaningful will always require you to say no to something else. That is the cost of creation. You cannot live in infinite possibility forever. At some point, you have to enter the arena. You have to pick up the pen, make the call, take the leap. Even if it is messy. Especially if it is messy.

You can do anything. But not everything. So stop waiting to feel ready. You will not. Start anyway. And when you fail, fail forward. Learn. Adjust. Continue.

Because the ones who go far are not always the most talented. They are the ones who keep going. Who stop romanticizing potential and start embracing reality.

And reality is this: you have to move. You have to begin. Or you will drown in all the things you could have been.

That is the paradox. Freedom without action becomes its own kind of prison. You are not trapped by limitations. You are trapped by the illusion that you have none.

So choose. Not perfectly. Not forever. But enough to get started.

Because if you can do anything, you must decide what is worth doing now.

The Spotlight Effect

The Echo of Judgment That Was Never Spoken

There is a psychological phenomenon that shapes the way many people move through the world, yet it often goes unnamed. It is not loud, but it echoes. It does not leave bruises, but it leaves hesitation. It is not always visible to others, but it feels overwhelming to the one experiencing it. It is called the spotlight effect. At its core, it is the belief that others are paying far more attention to you than they actually are. It is the quiet voice that tells you people noticed the stain on your shirt, the awkward way you walked into the room, or the slight crack in your voice during a presentation.

But the truth is, they rarely did.

Most people are too focused on themselves to truly notice the details of someone else's life. Yet the spotlight effect tricks the mind into thinking that the world is watching, that each mistake is being cataloged, that each decision is a moment of performance. The irony is that the fear of judgment becomes its own form of imprisonment. People hesitate to speak, to act, or to be seen as they are, all because of a perception that lives primarily in their own head.

This perception is not baseless. From an early age, many individuals are taught to seek approval. They are praised for doing well, and corrected for standing out in the wrong way. Over time, they begin to associate attention with evaluation. If someone is watching, it must mean they are judging. If someone is listening, it must mean they are waiting to find a flaw.

This creates a kind of internal surveillance. You become your own critic, your own observer, and your own warden. Every step, every action, and every word becomes something to overanalyze. Did I say the wrong thing? Did I come off as strange? Did I take up too much space? These questions echo long after the moment passes, long after anyone else has moved on.

In the modern world, this tendency has been amplified by the presence of digital media. Social platforms have transformed the average person into a curator of their own image. Every photo, every caption, every post is a decision about how to be perceived. The line between who someone is and who they appear to be becomes harder to draw. And when the line blurs, the spotlight brightens.

Now, people are not just imagining judgment. They are inviting it, fearing it, and living in response to it. The spotlight effect used to be internal. Now it is layered with likes, comments, and algorithms that decide what should be seen and what should be ignored. And yet, even with the increase in exposure, the same paradox remains: the world is not watching you nearly as much as you think.

This is where the echo begins. You imagine the spotlight is on you. You perform for it. You try to adjust, correct, improve. But most of the time, the audience you are performing for does not even exist.

This creates an exhausting pattern. You build your life around imagined expectations, trying to avoid embarrassment, rejection, or ridicule. But in doing so, you lose authenticity. You stop acting based on what you believe, and instead act based on what you think others believe. You lose sight of your own voice in an attempt to meet a standard that may not even be real.

The spotlight effect is not just a social fear. It is a paradox. It tells you that others are watching, but they are not. It tells you that your flaws are exposed, but they are forgotten. It tells you that the room is staring, when most eyes are fixed inward. People walk around with their own anxieties, their own regrets, their own spotlights blinding them from seeing anyone else clearly.

And yet, you carry yourself as if you are under constant observation. You hesitate to wear the outfit that feels right to you. You avoid sharing your ideas in a meeting. You stay silent when something important should be said. Not because anyone has told you not to, but because the spotlight has convinced you that it is safer to shrink than to stand out.

But is it safer?

What is the cost of living your life under a light that does not even exist? What opportunities are missed, what truths go unspoken, and what potential goes unseen because someone believed too strongly in the illusion of attention?

The spotlight effect does not only affect individuals. It shapes culture. It creates environments where people are more concerned with appearances than actions, with presentation than substance. It encourages conformity, because standing out feels dangerous. It breeds anxiety, because the fear of being judged becomes stronger than the desire to be understood.

This is the echo. Not of what others actually think, but of what you imagine they might think. It is the sound of your own self-doubt bouncing off the walls of your mind, made louder by silence.

But if you pause, if you take a step back, you may begin to see the illusion. Think about how often you notice the tiny details of someone else's mistake. Think about how long you remember the awkward moment someone else had. Think about how rarely you fixate on someone else's flaws. That is how often people think about you.

The paradox is simple. The more you believe others are watching, the more you hide. The more you hide, the less authentic you become. And the less authentic you become, the harder it is to be seen.

In truth, most people are too busy managing their own spotlight to focus on yours. They are worried about their own performance, their own mistakes, and their own echo of imagined judgment. The room is not filled with critics. It is filled with people who are too busy worrying about themselves to notice your flaws.

To escape this echo, you must begin to question the spotlight. Is it real? Or is it a projection? You must remind yourself that most people are more forgiving than you think. That silence is not judgment. That attention is not always criticism. That your mistakes are not magnified, they are just moments.

And if you begin to see the world this way, the echo fades. You start to act with more freedom. You speak more honestly. You move without constantly reviewing the tape in your head. You begin to trust that being seen is not the same as being condemned.

The spotlight was never real. The echo was never theirs.

It was yours.

Shame in a World That Forgets

Shame is one of the most powerful emotions a human can feel, yet it lives in a strange contradiction. It feels eternal when it strikes, as if a single moment of failure or exposure will follow us for the rest of our lives. And yet, the world that witnessed it rarely remembers. The paradox is this: we often carry the weight of shame long after everyone else has dropped it, assuming a spotlight remains on us long after it has turned elsewhere.

To feel shame is to believe that others are still watching. Not only watching, but judging, remembering, perhaps even laughing. It creates a fictional audience that lingers in the mind, an internal tribunal that recycles the same moments of humiliation, regret, or awkwardness. This imagined spotlight drives real decisions, alters behavior, and shapes identity, all in response to people who have long since moved on or never paid close attention to begin with.

In a world overwhelmed by information, the attention span of the average person has become incredibly short. People scroll past major headlines, forget viral scandals within days, and rarely notice the small mistakes of others. Yet we live as if every misstep we make is being recorded and replayed by a crowd. This cognitive dissonance makes shame uniquely durable. It survives not because others remember, but because we do. We rehearse our failures more often than anyone else ever will.

This phenomenon is amplified by the social structure we live in. School systems, corporate culture, and digital platforms all contain mechanisms of surveillance and feedback. A poor grade, a failed presentation, or a moment of awkwardness on social media can feel like a public collapse. But the truth is, people are mostly thinking about themselves. They are replaying their own mistakes, worrying about their own exposure. Shame tricks us into believing we are exceptions, that our errors are more visible, more memorable, and more defining than they actually are.

Even in the rare cases where shame is shared, such as in gossip or public commentary, the timeline of memory is unforgiving. Today's scandal becomes tomorrow's boredom. A society trained by content overload quickly forgets everything except the most sensational or repeated events. What feels like a defining moment to you may register as nothing to someone else. Still, the psychological impact remains, because shame is not about what they remember. It is about what we internalize.

There is another paradox inside shame: the more we try to forget it, the more we embed it. Avoidance becomes a rehearsal. We avoid people who were present during our low moments, we change our behavior to prevent future embarrassment, and in doing so we make the emotion stronger. Shame then becomes a filter through which we view all future situations. It shapes our sense of safety, confidence, and risk. It stops us from expressing ourselves, even when no one is watching.

The world is largely indifferent. Most people are too absorbed in their own lives to carry a detailed record of ours. Our minds, however, act as poor historians. We confuse emotional intensity with objective importance. If something felt horrible, we assume it was memorable. But memory does not work that way. Other people's recollection of our embarrassment is almost always weaker than we think. And even when they do remember, their judgment is fleeting, diluted by time and distraction.

Shame becomes most dangerous when it turns into identity. When a person begins to believe that their mistake is who they are, not just something they did, they carry that belief into every interaction. This creates a self-fulfilling cycle. We act smaller, we speak less, we step back. Others respond to that reduced presence, reinforcing the idea that we are not worthy. In reality, they are reacting to what we believe about ourselves, not to the original moment of shame. We become actors in a play written by our own insecurities.

There is a strange kind of freedom in realizing that most people are not thinking about you. This is not meant to be dismissive. It is meant to be liberating. You are not under constant review. The world is not a courtroom waiting to convict you for an awkward sentence, a failed attempt, or a wrong answer. People forget. They move on. And the few who do not are often carrying their own projections. Their judgment is more about them than it is about you.

This does not mean shame is not real. It is real. It is deeply felt. But it is often misplaced. It lingers in contexts where it no longer belongs. The challenge is not to erase it, but to confront it with clarity. To ask: who is really judging me, and how long will they remember? When you apply that question to the events you still carry with you, the answers are usually sobering. The memory is yours, but the audience is gone.

Some of the most powerful people in the world have made public mistakes. They have been caught in scandals, failures, and contradictions. And yet, many recover. They continue speaking, building, and living. Why? Because at some point, they understood that shame can only destroy you if you let it define you. It can only live in the shadows you refuse to enter. When brought into the light, it shrinks.

We live in a world that forgets quickly, yet we carry shame as if the world has perfect memory. That is the paradox. Shame is a heavy emotion in a world with no room to hold it. When you realize that, you begin to see that what haunts you is not what others remember. It is what you have not yet forgiven in yourself.

Invisible Eyes, Visible Pressure

There is a certain kind of weight that never announces itself, yet it is always there. It lingers quietly in social settings, in the way we dress, speak, and move through public space. It dictates the tone of our voice during meetings, the content of our posts online, even the things we do not say. This weight is not a person, or a rule, or a law. It is the idea of being watched. Not necessarily by someone specific, but by someone, anyone. The possibility that our actions are being observed at any given moment turns into a kind of invisible pressure that alters what we do, even when no one is there to see it.

This is the paradox of modern visibility. We live in an era where surveillance is not always imposed from the top down, but rather built into the structure of everyday life. Most people are not being watched by security cameras in a literal sense, but we act as though they are. Our digital footprints are permanent, and our social profiles are open windows. As a result, we begin to internalize the possibility of judgment. This judgment does not need to be active to be powerful. It only needs to be possible.

Even in private moments, people behave as though they are being evaluated. The mere anticipation of attention has replaced actual scrutiny. A person standing in front of a mirror rehearsing what they will say at work, or reviewing a text five times before hitting send, is not responding to current feedback. They are reacting to a future gaze, a potential response. This imagined audience becomes part of our psychology. Over time, it begins to shape our values, our decisions, and our comfort with risk.

There is a well-documented sociological phenomenon known as the panopticon. Originally designed as a theoretical prison, the panopticon placed a central watchtower in the middle of a circular building. Prisoners could not see whether the guard was watching them, but they knew the possibility was always there. As a result, they self-regulated their behavior. The brilliance of the design was not in constant surveillance, but in the threat of it. That concept has now been replicated in modern society, except the tower is not in the center of a prison. It is inside our minds.

We no longer need to be under direct observation to feel pressure. We simply need to believe that someone might be looking. The presence of cameras in public, the culture of sharing online, the normalization of feedback, and the viral nature of reputational collapse all contribute to this. The result is a society that polices itself, not through force, but through perceived observation. And the cost is that many people become afraid to act freely, not because someone is judging them, but because someone could be.

This kind of invisible pressure affects different people in different ways. For some, it creates a state of mild anxiety that runs in the background of daily life. They think carefully before expressing opinions, avoid speaking up in groups, or limit their online presence to what feels inoffensive. For others, the pressure becomes chronic, leading to perfectionism, burnout, or social withdrawal. The irony is that the fear of being judged does not need to be validated by actual feedback. The mind fills in the gaps. We imagine the worst possible response and adjust our behavior to avoid it.

This becomes even more complicated when the invisible eyes belong to people we know. The idea that friends, classmates, coworkers, or extended family are watching from a distance transforms our lives into ongoing performances. Every choice, from career decisions to relationship announcements to lifestyle habits, becomes a strategic act. We ask not only what we want, but how it will look. The internal question is no longer "Is this right for me?" but "What will they think if I do this?"

The pressure compounds when these observers are not neutral. If we know that someone disapproves of us, or once judged us in the past, we carry that expectation with us. We begin to censor ourselves, sometimes to the point of erasing parts of who we are. This is especially common in environments where identity, politics, or social status are closely monitored. People hide their real beliefs, change their outward personality, or even abandon their creative instincts to maintain appearances. And yet, many of the observers they fear are doing the same thing, equally afraid of being judged in return.

This shared performance becomes a paradox in itself. Everyone is pretending for each other, thinking that everyone else is more confident, more secure, more authentic. The truth is that many people are just as uncertain, just as constrained, and just as influenced by the invisible audience in their lives. The result is a culture where no one is truly themselves, and everyone assumes they are the only one holding back.

What makes this even more complicated is that many forms of pressure are now monetized. Influencers, public figures, and professionals often feel a financial dependency on staying within the lines of public acceptability. Their income, brand, or career opportunities may rely on remaining presentable to a wide range of observers. This is not just fear of judgment. It is fear of consequence. The stakes are higher, and the margin for error is narrower. In that context, the invisible eyes feel even more real. They do not just judge. They decide.

And yet, much like the earlier paradox of shame, this pressure often exists without active memory. People may notice a mistake, a misstep, or an awkward moment, but they rarely hold on to it. The human attention span is limited. Our capacity for outrage, disapproval, or fascination has a short half-life. This means the pressure we feel is often disproportionate to the reality of the social environment. But we respond to it anyway, because the potential of exposure is enough to silence action.

This shows up in small ways too. Someone hesitates before asking a question in a classroom or during a meeting, not because they are unsure of the question itself, but because they are afraid it will sound foolish. They picture a room full of eyes turning toward them, silently evaluating their intelligence. So they stay silent, reinforcing the very thing they feared, the appearance of disengagement. Meanwhile, others in the room may be wishing someone would speak up, or feeling the exact same fear themselves.

This invisible pressure also plays a role in creativity. People with ideas, art, or opinions often hesitate to share them because of an imagined critic who will tear them down. They preemptively silence their originality to avoid hypothetical disapproval. This prevents innovation, growth, and contribution. It turns creative spaces into quiet ones, where the loudest voices are often the least reflective, and the most thoughtful people remain unheard.

As the pressure to appear correct grows, the space for experimentation shrinks. In science, business, art, and conversation, mistakes are an essential part of progress. But the fear of being judged for those mistakes causes people to take fewer risks. They stay close to the consensus, imitate others, or recycle safe ideas. This leads to stagnation, both personally and culturally. We create a society of safe thinkers who are afraid to explore the unknown, not because they lack ideas, but because they fear being seen trying.

The most powerful solution to this invisible pressure is not rebellion, but awareness. Once you recognize the pattern, you can begin to resist its grip. You can question the audience in your head and ask whether it truly exists. You can take small steps toward honesty, vulnerability, and imperfection, knowing that most people are not thinking about you as much as you think they are. And even if they are, their thoughts are fleeting.

There is something radical about authenticity in a world of performance. Not because it is loud or confrontational, but because it is rare. When someone speaks plainly, acts freely, or admits uncertainty, they disrupt the cycle of silent conformity. They remind others that it is possible to live without constantly watching yourself. That courage creates space for others to do the same.

This invisible pressure becomes most dangerous when it attaches itself to relationships. Romantic connections, friendships, and even family ties are not immune to the gaze we project into the world. A person may hesitate to express how they feel because they imagine being perceived as needy, weak, or irrational. This imagined perception is not coming from their partner or friend directly, but from an invisible third-party audience — a collection of expectations, social rules, and stereotypes absorbed over time. They do not want to seem like the person who cares too much, so they say nothing, even when they are aching to be understood.

This effect becomes more prominent when others are physically present but emotionally distant. For example, you may be sitting in a room full of people, yet feel completely watched and entirely alone at the same time. The sense that you must behave a certain way, stay composed, avoid being too loud or too quiet, becomes overwhelming. You are surrounded, yet scrutinized. You are included, yet pressured to prove that inclusion was deserved. Even in moments of supposed connection, the invisible audience creates disconnection. It replaces real interaction with performance.

Social media magnifies this experience by a hundredfold. Online platforms are built on the assumption of observation. Every post, photo, or comment is made with an audience in mind. The lines between communication and broadcasting blur. Even mundane updates are now filtered through the question: how will this make me look? And because so many others are doing the same thing, we begin to measure our lives not by what they mean, but by how they appear.

The algorithm becomes the spotlight. It rewards what is popular, reacts to what is dramatic, and suppresses what is thoughtful but quiet. People adjust their behavior to match this logic. They post not what is real, but what is rewarded. Over time, the pressure to be seen as successful, happy, attractive, or socially desirable becomes embedded in their self-image. And yet, no one can ever fully live up to that performance, so they begin to feel like impostors in their own curated lives.

This creates another paradox, we are more visible than ever before, and yet we feel less known. The pressure to maintain a specific version of ourselves makes authenticity rare and vulnerability expensive. People compare themselves not to real others, but to polished illusions. They imagine being watched by peers, rivals, and strangers alike, all waiting for them to slip. The pressure does not come from any one person, but from the collective idea that someone, somewhere, is keeping score.

And the scoreboard is always invisible. There is no official feedback. You never really know what others think. But the fear of being misjudged or misunderstood is enough to make you preemptively change yourself. This becomes exhausting. It drains mental energy, increases self-consciousness, and diminishes joy. You no longer do things just because they matter to you. You do them while wondering how others will interpret them, how they will fit into your image, how they will be judged by people you may never meet.

Technology does not just amplify this effect, it codifies it. Facial recognition, biometric tracking, engagement metrics, and digital records all contribute to a sense of constant traceability. Every move, every click, every typed message is stored somewhere. You do not need to be famous or important to be indexed by the system. Simply existing online makes you part of the machine. As a result, people begin to self-censor in increasingly subtle ways. They post less, speak less, experiment less. The digital environment becomes a carefully polished gallery of safe personas.

Even privacy becomes performative. People announce when they are taking a break from social media, as if stepping away must be justified. Others create private accounts just to escape the pressure of their main profile. Some turn to anonymous spaces, hoping to rediscover the freedom of unfiltered thought. But even there, the invisible eyes follow. The fear that what is said in secret will one day be exposed prevents true openness. We begin to fear not just judgment in the present, but exposure in the future.

This fear changes the way we learn. Students, employees, and even leaders are often reluctant to admit they do not know something. Asking questions becomes a risk. It suggests incompetence, and in a world where reputations are fragile, people avoid that risk. So they nod along, pretend to understand, and leave the room more confused than when they entered. The cost of visibility is ignorance. People stop learning because they are too busy performing.

The effect is cumulative. Over time, the person you present to the world becomes more practiced than the person you are in private. Your voice changes. Your interests narrow. Your personality adapts to what is expected. And eventually, the real you feels like a ghost, faint, buried under layers of presentation. You no longer ask what you want. You ask what others want from you. You become a projection of what you believe others will accept.

And yet, the truth is that the audience is not as active as we think. Most people are absorbed in their own inner worlds. They are worried about how they look, what others think of them, how they will be perceived. They are not watching you. They are watching themselves. The invisible eyes you feel are often mirrors of your own mind. You imagine being judged because you have judged yourself first.

There is a freedom in remembering this. Not because it means you can act without consequence, but because it means you can act without pretense. You do not need to be invisible to feel free. You simply need to stop giving power to the imagined observers who are not truly present. The pressure to be perfect, acceptable, admired, or aligned is a weight you are allowed to put down.

Some of the greatest acts of authenticity are not loud declarations. They are small choices made in silence. Choosing to speak honestly even when your voice shakes. Sharing something real even when it is not polished. Asking a question when you do not know the answer. Admitting uncertainty in a world that worships certainty. These acts break the illusion of the invisible audience. They remind others that freedom is possible, not by disappearing, but by refusing to perform.

And when one person does that, others follow. Vulnerability is contagious in the best way. When someone speaks without fear of judgment, they create space for others to do the same. The room becomes lighter. The masks begin to fall. And what is left is not chaos, but connection. Real connection. The kind that cannot exist under the pressure of invisible eyes.

The Audience That Got It Wrong

There is a strange discomfort in knowing that you are being seen, but not being seen clearly. The spotlight effect is not only about being watched. It is about being watched through the wrong lens. You are observed, evaluated, remembered, but inaccurately. You carry the burden of their impressions, even when those impressions are shallow, distorted, or incomplete. And yet, they still affect you. This is the paradox: your identity is influenced by perceptions that are neither true nor permanent.

Every person carries an internal story of who they are. It is built from memory, thought, desire, and reflection. But that private story is often interrupted by a louder, external narrative, the one others write for you. They interpret a glance, a silence, a single comment, and from it, they build an assumption. That assumption may be entirely wrong, but it becomes part of how they respond to you. And how they respond to you begins to shape how you behave. So even if their version is incorrect, it has power.

This is where the trap forms. You start to feel obligated to correct that version of yourself. You notice when someone thinks you are shy, when you are just quiet. When someone thinks you are arrogant, when you are just guarded. When someone calls you distant, when you are just overwhelmed. And instead of staying rooted in your actual self, you begin reacting to their misunderstanding. You perform not to express who you are, but to prove who you are not.

This reaction becomes exhausting. You are not living freely. You are managing impressions. You are cleaning up misconceptions, editing your behavior, and anticipating what others might get wrong next. It becomes a full-time job, the job of constantly updating the version of yourself that lives in other people's minds. But no matter how carefully you manage it, the audience always gets something wrong. Because their view of you is limited by their own filters, their own biases, past experiences, and insecurities. You become less of a person to them and more of a projection.

This is especially true in the early stages of relationships. First impressions are rarely accurate, yet they stick with surprising force. A single awkward moment can become your defining trait in someone's mind. A joke taken the wrong way, a pause misread as disinterest, a facial expression interpreted as coldness, all of it becomes part of the version they remember. And once that version is formed, it becomes resistant to change. You are locked into their mental file, even if it does not resemble the truth.

The danger is not just that others get it wrong. It is that you begin to doubt yourself. If enough people see you a certain way, you start to wonder if they are right. You second guess your motives, your confidence, your worth. You begin to treat their perception as evidence. This is a slow erosion of the self. You chip away at your instincts, your voice, your expression, all to fit into a shape that was never yours to begin with.

This happens in both subtle and visible ways. Someone who is constantly called sensitive may stop speaking up, even when something truly bothers them. A person labeled too intense may begin shrinking their ambition. Someone misunderstood as arrogant may start over-explaining themselves to appear humble. And the tragedy is that none of these changes address the root problem. They are efforts to fix a misunderstanding that was never theirs to fix.

The audience that got it wrong still holds the power to alter your reality. In schools, this can come from teachers who misunderstand a student's quietness as disengagement. In the workplace, it can come from a boss who mistakes calm confidence for lack of drive. In social circles, it can come from peers who define you by one moment instead of a larger pattern. And once that misreading takes hold, it becomes hard to rewrite. The human mind is more likely to defend a first impression than to revise it.

Public perception, especially in the age of digital profiles, accelerates this problem. Online, there is less room for nuance. Posts, comments, and curated images are interpreted quickly and often harshly. A single sentence taken out of context can become a defining moment. A video clip can erase years of consistent behavior. In this environment, the risk of being misunderstood grows exponentially. And when that misunderstanding spreads, it feels as though the audience has multiplied.

You are now not only reacting to one person's version of you, but to the collective assumption of thousands. Even if those assumptions are shallow, they shape opportunity. They shape inclusion. They shape who is invited, who is heard, and who is dismissed. The person you know yourself to be may never get the chance to show up, because the room has already been convinced otherwise.

This is one of the most difficult parts of being human, knowing yourself, but not being seen as that person. It is not just frustrating. It is isolating. You begin to feel invisible in the one way that matters most: not unseen, but unseen accurately. And while you can argue against what people say, it is much harder to argue against what people assume. Because assumptions are quiet. They are not always spoken out loud. They live in tone, in timing, in the way someone answers your message or fails to invite you to something. You are reacting to signals, not statements.

And still, you feel the need to respond. You want to prove them wrong. But trying to prove yourself often makes things worse.

It can look like overcompensation. It can come off as insecurity. The more you try to escape the wrong version of yourself, the more it becomes the focus of your identity. You are no longer living, you are correcting. And correction is not connection. It is defense.

Real connection only begins when both people are willing to drop their assumptions. When they are curious instead of certain. When they ask questions instead of making silent conclusions. But that kind of interaction requires emotional maturity, patience, and trust, qualities that are increasingly rare in fast-paced social environments. Most people do not take the time to know who you really are. They settle for a quick label. And you are left carrying the weight of it.

The solution is not to make yourself invisible, and it is not to spend your life defending yourself. It is to return to your own definition. To re-anchor your identity in something deeper than public impressions. This does not mean you ignore feedback. It means you learn to separate useful insight from lazy assumptions. Some people will misunderstand you no matter what you do. Their version of you is built more from their own story than from yours.

And when that happens, you must learn to let them be wrong. Not because you do not care, but because you cannot live your life trying to fix a lens that is not yours to adjust. You do not owe every stranger an explanation. You do not owe every critic your energy. The cost of proving yourself to everyone is the loss of yourself to no one in particular.

Freedom begins when you no longer perform for people who are not paying attention. It begins when you stop rehearsing responses for those who are not listening. It begins when you accept that being misunderstood is not always a crisis. Sometimes it is just a reflection of the limits of human perception. The audience got it wrong. That is not your burden to carry forever.

When someone misunderstands you, their version of you often says more about them than it does about you. A person who grew up around anger may mistake firmness for hostility. Someone who feels insecure might interpret confidence as arrogance. A person who struggles with trust may assume silence means deception. You become a mirror, reflecting back whatever unprocessed story they are carrying. Their version of you is built from fragments of themselves.

But here is where the paradox deepens. Even when you understand that someone's perception of you is inaccurate, it still affects you. Logic alone does not erase the emotional weight of being misread. You can tell yourself it does not matter, that their opinion is flawed, that their assumptions are unfair. But their version still lives in the room. It still shapes how they treat you. And being treated as someone you are not can begin to erode the version of yourself you are trying to protect.

People who are constantly misunderstood often develop emotional armor. They become careful. They filter what they say. They anticipate criticism and adjust accordingly. Over time, this turns into a kind of internal distortion. You begin to lose the sharpness of your self-definition, not because you do not know who you are, but because you have become accustomed to softening your presence to survive in spaces where you are misread.

This can be especially damaging for people who exist at the margins of society. Those whose identities do not conform to cultural expectations — whether because of race, gender, neurodivergence, or personality — are often the most misunderstood. They are told, explicitly or implicitly, that their natural way of being is too much, or not enough, or wrong altogether. And so they shape-shift. They become palatable. They try to fit into containers that were not made for them. But the more they do this, the more they disconnect from themselves.

Being seen inaccurately over and over again begins to feel like erasure. You walk into a room knowing exactly who you are, and you leave feeling as though you were not even there. The version that people reacted to was never yours. It was theirs. And yet you are the one who has to carry the confusion. You are the one left wondering how to navigate a world that cannot or will not see you clearly.

This is not just a personal problem. It is a social and structural one. Institutions are built on perception. Who is hired, who is promoted, who is included, all of it is influenced by how people are perceived. And if perception is flawed, then access becomes flawed. People are denied opportunities not because they lack talent or character, but because the gatekeepers got the story wrong. They evaluated the surface, not the substance. They judged from a distance, then made decisions with lasting impact.

In moments like these, the desire to prove oneself becomes overwhelming. You want to break through the distortion. You want to show them the truth. But this can become a trap. The more you focus on proving who you are, the more your energy is spent on performance instead of creation. You begin to live in reaction to their version of you, instead of building your life from your own foundation.

There is a quiet kind of rebellion in choosing not to correct every misconception. It is not indifference. It is clarity. It is the understanding that not every version of you deserves your time. Some people will misunderstand you because they are not ready to see clearly. Others will do so because it is easier to reduce than to understand. And some will see only what serves their story. You cannot spend your life negotiating with every broken lens. At some point, you have to stop explaining and start living.

This does not mean you give up on being understood. It means you begin to value where that understanding actually happens. You look for the rare people who are willing to ask, to listen, to pause before concluding. You invest in the spaces where your complexity is not a threat, but an invitation. In those spaces, identity can breathe. You are allowed to be layered. You are allowed to be in progress. You are allowed to change.

The pressure to be understood by everyone is a subtle form of perfectionism. It says that your worth is tied to your clarity in the eyes of others. But clarity is not always possible. Some people will only ever see you through the fog of their own expectations. That is not a reflection of your value. It is a reflection of their limitations.

The paradox is that sometimes, the more you try to be understood, the more misunderstood you become. Explanation can be twisted. Vulnerability can be weaponized. Honesty can be reframed as manipulation. You give people the tools to understand you, but if they are not ready to use them, they will misuse them. This is why wisdom often involves knowing when to speak and when to stay silent. When to clarify, and when to walk away.

The audience that got it wrong may never update their version of you. They may cling to it, because it serves their pride, their certainty, or their narrative. But you do not need their permission to evolve. You do not need their approval to be whole. What matters more than being understood is being real. And being real sometimes means living with the fact that others will not see you clearly.

It is painful, but it is also freeing. Because once you stop chasing their version of you, you begin to deepen your connection with your own. You stop splitting yourself into fragments to satisfy an audience that was never listening closely. You begin to write your own narrative, not for applause, but for alignment. Not for validation, but for truth.

Some people will never understand who you are, even if you show them everything. Others will see you before you speak a word. That difference is not random. It is the result of their own openness, their own sensitivity, their own depth. You cannot control it. But you can choose where to stand. And you can choose to stand fully in the light of your own reality, whether they recognize it or not.

The world will always have more spectators than listeners. More people looking at you than into you. The goal is not to make them see. The goal is not to adjust yourself so they are comfortable. The goal is to live in such a way that, whether they understand you or not, you remain yourself.

The hedonic treadmill

The Chase That Never Ends

There is a feeling that most people have experienced, even if they have never named it. It arrives after something good, a promotion, a new relationship, a better apartment, a long-awaited vacation. In that moment, the world feels lighter. You feel seen, accomplished, or simply fortunate. You believe that things will feel different now. That this, finally, will change everything. But time passes, and the feeling fades. What was once new becomes normal. What once sparked joy becomes part of the background. And before long, your mind begins to wonder, what is next?

This cycle is not random. It is part of how human emotion functions. Our minds are not wired to stay in extremes. We return to a kind of emotional baseline, even after major events. That baseline might shift slightly over time, depending on your health, relationships, or environment. But the general pattern remains. We adapt. And because we adapt, we keep chasing. We seek out the next improvement, the next change, the next high. It becomes a loop. A chase that never ends.

This concept has a name in psychology. It is called hedonic adaptation, sometimes referred to as the hedonic treadmill. The term describes the way people quickly adjust to improved circumstances. Whether it is more money, more success, or more freedom, the emotional effect is temporary. You feel happier for a short period, but then your expectations catch up. What once made you feel rich now feels average. What once seemed exciting now seems routine. And so, you search for something new to elevate your happiness again.

The metaphor of the treadmill is important. You are running, exerting effort, moving forward, but you remain in the same emotional place. Your external life might improve dramatically, but your internal state resets. You do not feel significantly more content. You might even feel frustrated that the improvement did not satisfy you the way you hoped it would. And so, the chase continues.

This is not a failure of character. It is part of the human brain's survival system. From an evolutionary standpoint, the ability to adapt was useful. It kept people alert, ambitious, and resourceful. But in the modern world, where many people are no longer focused on physical survival, this adaptation mechanism works against emotional well-being. It keeps happiness just out of reach, no matter how much progress is made.

This shows up clearly in material pursuits. A person may work hard to buy their first car, feel thrilled, and then within months begin dreaming of a newer model. A couple may move into a larger home, feel proud, and then soon begin noticing its flaws. An individual might finally reach a six-figure income, only to start comparing themselves to those earning twice as much. The finish line moves. The feeling fades. The goal is achieved, but the contentment does not last.

Even relationships are affected by this adaptation. The early stages of connection are often full of energy, fascination, and emotional intensity. But over time, the novelty wears off. People settle into routines. The things they once adored about each other become invisible or even irritating. They begin to fantasize about other possibilities, forgetting that the same pattern will likely repeat. Newness is not sustainable, but the chase for it remains.

People are constantly exposed to images of lifestyles that appear more glamorous, exciting, or fulfilling. This creates a feedback loop of comparison. Even if someone is content, seeing others with more can create the sense that something is missing. You were happy with your vacation until you saw someone else's trip. You liked your apartment until you saw someone else's loft. The baseline moves not because your reality changed, but because your reference point did.

This constant comparison feeds into the treadmill effect. You are no longer just adapting to your own progress. You are adapting to the visible progress of others. And since people often only share highlights, you are chasing a version of success that is curated, not real. The result is a quiet dissatisfaction that builds over time. You feel like you are not keeping up, even if you are objectively doing well. You feel like you are behind, even when you are far ahead of where you started.

The paradox here is that most of the things people chase are not inherently bad. It is not wrong to want a better job, a stable home, or meaningful achievement. The issue is not the desire for improvement. It is the belief that improvement will fix everything. That once you arrive at a certain level, happiness will settle in and stay. But it rarely does. Because the mind recalibrates. The satisfaction window closes, and you find yourself wanting again.

This is why some people become addicted to chasing goals. Not because they are shallow, but because they have built their identity around forward motion. They do not know how to rest. They do not know how to enjoy themselves. Every accomplishment is quickly replaced with the next target. They are successful on paper, but emotionally restless. Their life becomes a resume of victories with very few moments of stillness. And if they try to slow down, they feel lost.

Others take a different path. They stop chasing entirely. Burned by the pattern, they conclude that nothing will ever bring lasting happiness, so they disengage. They abandon goals, avoid risk, and detach from ambition. But this too is a trap. It replaces the illusion of eternal progress with the illusion of permanent detachment. It assumes that desire must be eliminated, rather than understood.

The more sustainable path lies somewhere in the middle. It involves recognizing the treadmill without pretending it does not exist. You acknowledge that your brain will adapt. You understand that the high will fade. But you do not build your life around chasing the high. Instead, you begin to anchor meaning in things that do not disappear when the excitement does.

This includes relationships that deepen over time, even as the novelty fades. Work that challenges you, even when it is not glamorous. A sense of purpose that is not tied to applause or comparison. Gratitude for stability, even when it is not exciting. These things do not create constant happiness, but they create a steadiness that does not collapse with every mood shift.

There is also power in learning to recognize the moment when the chase has returned. That moment when a recent success no longer feels satisfying, and your mind begins searching again. If you catch it early, you can pause. You can ask whether the next thing is truly necessary, or just another attempt to escape the feeling of neutrality. Because neutrality is not failure. It is where most of life happens. It is the space between extremes, and it deserves to be respected.

We live in a culture that rarely celebrates neutrality. It values peaks. It rewards novelty. It praises movement. And because of that, people feel pressure to constantly upgrade. To constantly strive. To constantly chase. But there is wisdom in slowing down, in noticing that what you have now was once what you wanted most. There is peace in realizing that the next level will not save you. It will only reset you.

Still, this realization is difficult to hold onto. The world does not stop suggesting that you are behind. Algorithms, advertisements, and social circles will all continue pointing you toward the next thing. And you will continue to feel the pull. That is natural. What matters is whether you chase with awareness, or out of habit. Whether you move forward because it aligns with your values, or because you are afraid to stand still.

The chase itself is not wrong. It becomes dangerous when you forget that it will never end. When you believe that happiness is waiting at the finish line. When you confuse progress with fulfillment. Fulfillment requires presence. It requires reflection. It requires stepping off the treadmill long enough to realize that you are not required to earn your right to be content.

There will always be another goal. Another purchase. Another milestone. The world will never run out of things to offer you. But none of them will offer you permanent peace. That is not because peace is impossible. It is because peace does not come from arrival. It comes from recognizing that even without the next thing, you are still allowed to feel whole.

The language people use often reveals how deeply the chase is ingrained. You hear phrases like "when I get there," "once I make it," or "after I have enough." But these statements rarely refer to a specific destination. They are placeholders for a state of emotional security that never arrives. Because "there" keeps moving. "Enough" is redefined. And what once felt far away becomes the new minimum.

Even among those who have achieved extraordinary things, the chase does not disappear. Many of the world's most visibly successful individuals continue pushing for more — not because they are greedy, but because stillness feels foreign. The applause fades. The recognition fades. The satisfaction fades. And they are left with the same question that fueled them from the beginning: what now?

This is not limited to money or status. It shows up in personal growth as well. A person who becomes more confident may soon feel pressure to become more charismatic. Someone who heals from trauma may begin striving for total emotional balance. A person who has made great progress in one area begins to feel lacking in another. The moment one need is fulfilled, another emerges. Growth becomes a series of moving targets, none of which produce lasting stillness.

The modern self-help industry, despite its positive intentions, often reinforces this. It offers strategies for constant improvement, endless productivity, and limitless potential. While these ideas can be helpful, they can also create the illusion that contentment is something you have to earn. That you are not allowed to be satisfied until you have optimized every part of your life. That rest is only acceptable once you have completed an invisible checklist.

But this checklist never ends. There is always more to fix, more to change, more to achieve. And if you accept that framework, you begin to view yourself as a constant project. Not a person, but a problem to be solved. This creates pressure, not peace. It keeps your attention on what is lacking, not on what is present. It turns your life into a draft that is never ready to be published.

The hedonic treadmill is not just a theory. It is a trap that millions of people walk into without realizing it. It is disguised as ambition, but it is rooted in restlessness. It is disguised as progress, but it is driven by dissatisfaction. And because it looks productive from the outside, it is rarely questioned. People admire the ones who never stop moving. They rarely ask whether that movement is voluntary, or whether it is just a desperate attempt to feel enough.

There are moments, though, when the illusion cracks. Moments when the chase feels hollow. You achieve something you worked hard for, but the celebration feels forced. You reach a milestone you thought would change you, but you still feel like the same person. You stand on a stage, receive an award, or move into the home you once dreamed about — and you feel a strange silence inside. Not sadness, but absence. The feeling you expected is not there.

These moments are not failures. They are invitations. They are reminders that the structure of your happiness might need to change. That you have been running for so long, you forgot why you started. That your goals have become habits, not desires. That your movement is no longer taking you where you want to go.

This is when reflection becomes essential. Not the shallow kind that asks, "What is next?" but the deeper kind that asks, "Why do I keep needing a next?" This question is not meant to end ambition. It is meant to realign it. To separate what is truly meaningful from what is simply familiar. Because sometimes, the chase continues not because you want what is next, but because you do not know what to do without a chase.

This addiction to movement is not always obvious. It hides behind achievement, discipline, and routine. It looks responsible. But it prevents people from sitting still long enough to experience peace. And peace requires stillness. It requires presence. It requires the ability to enjoy where you are without immediately reaching for where you are not.

Some cultures understand this better than others. In societies that prioritize community, ritual, and slow living, people often report higher levels of life satisfaction despite lower levels of material wealth. That is not because they lack ambition. It is because they have learned to value things that do not vanish when you get used to them. Connection, purpose, rhythm, these do not fade in the way that new toys or titles do.

Modern society, by contrast, is built on acceleration. New is better. Fast is better. More is better. But none of these things address the deeper emotional need for contentment. And so, even as the world becomes more advanced, more efficient, and more connected, people report feeling more anxious, more isolated, and more restless. The treadmill moves faster, but the destination remains the same.

The hardest part about escaping the treadmill is that doing so often feels like giving up. If you stop chasing, you might worry that you are being lazy, unmotivated, or complacent. But there is a difference between giving up and stepping off. Giving up is when you let go because you are defeated. Stepping off is when you let go because you have realized the game is not worth playing in the same way anymore.

Stepping off the treadmill does not mean abandoning progress. It means redefining it. It means choosing goals that align with your values, not just your status. It means moving toward what matters, not just what looks impressive. It means learning to stay in moments of peace without ruining them with anticipation of the next goal.

The people who live with the most peace are not always the ones with the least ambition. They are the ones who have made peace with the fact that ambition will never satisfy the deeper questions of existence. That growth is good, but it is not everything. That success is valuable, but it is not salvation. That happiness is not a finish line. It is a rhythm. And sometimes, it plays quietly.

If you find yourself chasing again, pause. Ask whether the next thing is solving a problem, or distracting from one. Ask whether you are moving out of inspiration or out of habit. Ask whether you can stay where you are, not forever, but for now. And if the answer is no, ask why.

Because in the end, the chase is only endless if you never question it. The treadmill keeps moving only if you keep running without looking around. But the moment you stop, the moment you look inward instead of forward, the world slows down. And in that space, you may find something you have not felt in a long time. Not excitement. Not pride. But rest.

The Happiness That Never Stays

Happiness is one of the most sought-after states in the world. People plan their lives around it. They pursue careers, build relationships, accumulate experiences, and acquire possessions in the name of it. Every major decision, from what job to take to where to live to who to marry, is influenced by the question: will this make me happy? And yet, for something that holds so much power over human behavior, happiness remains painfully unstable. It arrives in flashes, and disappears without warning. It lifts the spirit one day and fades into silence the next. You reach for it again, but it never seems to stay.

This emotional impermanence is not accidental. It is deeply tied to the structure of the human brain. Emotions, by nature, are designed to fluctuate. They are signals, not destinations. Joy, excitement, pride, and contentment are part of a much larger emotional ecosystem. If happiness were permanent, it would cease to have meaning. It would become invisible, just another part of the background. The contrast is what gives it value. The rise is only felt because there is a fall.

But knowing this does not make it easier to live with. Most people expect happiness to last longer than it does. They believe that once certain conditions are met, it should settle in. That with the right job, the right partner, the right place to live, happiness will finally become the default. And when it does not, they assume something is wrong. They question the choices they made, or worse, they begin to believe they are incapable of being happy for long. But the issue is not with their decisions or their wiring. It is with the expectation that happiness should be permanent.

This expectation is fueled by the way happiness is portrayed. In films, books, and advertisements, it is often shown as a lasting state. Characters find love, overcome adversity, or reach success, and the story ends there, as if the happiness that follows will never fade. But real life does not stop at the peak. It continues. The same people who were once overjoyed return to normal life. The same problems reappear in different forms. The emotional high levels out. And if you were told that happiness was supposed to stay, this feels like a betrayal.

There is also a cultural narrative that treats unhappiness as a problem to be fixed. If you are not happy, something must be wrong. You must have made the wrong choice, or failed to optimize your life properly. You must need a new routine, a new habit, a new mindset. And so people chase fixes. They look for books, courses, and frameworks that promise emotional stability. But happiness is not a technical issue. It is not something that can be installed like a program. It is a moving state, and it cannot be frozen in place without losing its essence.

The paradox is that the harder you try to hold onto happiness, the faster it slips through your fingers. It resists being possessed. It cannot be pinned down or scheduled. It often arrives when you are not looking for it, during a quiet moment, a kind word, a small victory. And it often leaves when you begin to expect it most. The pressure to be happy can become a source of stress in itself. People feel guilty for not feeling good, even when their circumstances suggest they should. They are surrounded by reasons to feel joy, yet feel nothing. And this emotional dissonance can be devastating.

This is where the idea of hedonic adaptation becomes relevant again. The same mechanism that dulls the excitement of new experiences also blunts the intensity of happiness over time. What once brought joy now feels neutral. What once inspired awe now feels familiar. The human brain is designed to normalize its environment, which means that even the most beautiful moments eventually become background noise if they repeat often enough. You cannot feel wonder at something you see every day. And yet, that thing may still be remarkable. It is your perception that has changed.

This does not mean that happiness is meaningless. It means that happiness is fragile. It is something to be experienced, not something to be owned. It is a guest, not a tenant. And like any guest, it must be welcomed when it arrives and released when it leaves. Trying to trap it only leads to resentment. You begin to see happiness as a requirement, rather than a gift. You stop noticing its presence, and start focusing only on its absence.

People often look back on their happiest times with a kind of nostalgia that is tinted by pain. Not just because the moments are gone, but because they did not realize how good they were while they were happening. This is another layer of the paradox. You do not always know you are happy until the moment passes. Your awareness lags behind your experience. And by the time you catch up, the conditions have changed.

There are ways to lengthen the presence of happiness, but they are not what most people expect. They do not come from more success, more stimulation, or more control. They come from attention. From the ability to notice the good without needing it to last. From the ability to feel joy without gripping it so tightly that it breaks. Gratitude, mindfulness, and humility are tools not for chasing happiness, but for holding it gently. They do not make happiness permanent. They make it easier to remember.

One of the dangers of expecting happiness to stay is that it causes people to panic when it leaves. They begin to unravel what was once a positive experience, trying to figure out where things went wrong. They create narratives of loss where there is only emotional transition. Instead of recognizing that the shift is natural, they blame themselves or others. A good relationship that loses its spark is declared a failure. A meaningful job that feels dull after a year is seen as a mistake. But the change in feeling is not proof of failure. It is proof of being human.

Some of the most meaningful experiences in life are not joyful in the conventional sense. They are difficult, but rich. Challenging, but purposeful. Emotional, but not easy. Raising children, building something from nothing, caring for someone in illness, these moments are not filled with constant happiness. But they carry depth. They matter in ways that go beyond mood. If you measure your life only by how often you feel good, you miss the full story. You reduce life to a chart of highs and lows, forgetting that some of the most valuable moments exist in the middle.

The idea that happiness should stay also creates unrealistic expectations in relationships. Partners often expect each other to be a source of constant joy, and when the emotional intensity fades, they assume the relationship is broken. But relationships are not designed to sustain peak emotion. They are meant to evolve. The early thrill of discovery gives way to the slower rhythm of trust, intimacy, and shared experience. That rhythm does not always feel exciting, but it can feel deeply fulfilling, if you are not expecting it to match the emotional spikes of the beginning.

The same is true for personal growth. The initial burst of motivation that comes from starting something new will not last forever. The gym loses its novelty. The journal becomes repetitive. The diet feels restrictive. And when the happiness fades, many people stop. They assume that without the emotional high, the action is no longer worth it. But some of the most important habits in life are built not during moments of happiness, but in the quiet that follows.

This is the paradox at the heart of emotional maturity: learning to keep going even when the happiness is gone. Not because you are numb or robotic, but because you understand that meaning lasts longer than mood. You do not abandon the path just because the scenery becomes familiar. You keep moving, knowing that happiness may return, or it may not. But either way, your life is still worth living.

Even deeper than the expectation of happiness is the fear of its opposite. Many people fear sadness, loneliness, boredom, or discomfort so intensely that they chase happiness not for its own sake, but to escape the alternative. This turns happiness into a defense mechanism, not a true experience. It becomes something they pursue out of fear, not out of joy. And because it is fear-based, it can never truly satisfy.

True happiness cannot be forced. It cannot be scheduled. It emerges in moments that are often quiet, unplanned, and free from pressure. It appears when you are not trying to extract it. When you are fully engaged in what you are doing, not because it will make you happy, but because it matters. Happiness then becomes a side effect, not a goal. And like all side effects, it is unpredictable. But it is also more honest.

When happiness is misunderstood, people also misinterpret its fragility. They treat its disappearance as personal failure, rather than natural transition. But happiness often fades not because something is wrong, but because the conditions that once produced it have changed. And sometimes, those conditions are not external. They are internal.

One of the most overlooked reasons happiness does not last is because people are rarely prepared to hold it. They spend so much time pursuing happiness that they do not develop the emotional capacity to carry it. The mind becomes used to striving, solving, and fixing. When there is nothing left to fix, it feels strange. Calm can feel unfamiliar. Joy can feel suspicious. Peace can feel like a setup for disappointment. In those moments, people begin to self-sabotage, not consciously, but out of discomfort with the stillness happiness brings.

This is especially common in individuals who have lived with chronic stress or emotional volatility. For them, happiness feels fragile, almost dangerous. They wait for something to go wrong. They question whether the joy is real. Their nervous system does not trust the good moment to last. And so they create distance from it. They underplay their success. They mute their joy. They return to worry, because worry feels more familiar than contentment. The emotional system rejects what it was never trained to receive.

Another factor that makes happiness hard to hold is overstimulation. In modern life, people are exposed to a constant stream of information, entertainment, and novelty. Their senses are always occupied. Their minds are rarely still. This makes it difficult for happiness to register fully. Moments of genuine joy are interrupted by digital distractions. Attention is fractured. Presence is rare. And without presence, even the most beautiful experiences can pass by unnoticed.

There is a kind of numbness that develops when everything is always available. It is no longer enough to eat a good meal, it must be photographed, reviewed, and compared to others. It is no longer enough to travel somewhere beautiful, it must be documented and shared. These layers of performance separate people from the core feeling of the moment. They are happy, but their attention is elsewhere. And so the happiness dissolves before it fully settles in.

Some people also experience happiness as guilt. They question whether they deserve to feel good, especially if others around them are struggling. They worry that joy makes them selfish, out of touch, or insensitive. And so they quiet it. They do not allow themselves to celebrate. They do not speak openly about their success or gratitude. They keep it small, as if to apologize for it. In doing so, they make happiness conditional on suffering. They refuse to feel good unless everyone else does too.

This moral framing of emotion becomes a burden. People treat joy like a luxury they must earn. They do not allow themselves to feel it fully unless every aspect of their life, and the world, is in order. But that day will never come. There will always be imperfection, conflict, and pain. Waiting for the absence of suffering before allowing joy means that joy will never be fully felt. It is possible to hold both, to care about others and still be allowed to experience happiness.

Another reason happiness does not stay is that people do not know how to let it evolve. They expect it to keep feeling the same way it did in the beginning. But like any emotion, happiness changes form. What once felt like excitement may later feel like peace. What began as celebration may turn into appreciation. These are not lesser states. They are deeper ones. But if someone is only looking for the emotional high, they may miss the quiet contentment that follows.

This is why so many people confuse happiness with intensity. They associate it with loud laughter, high energy, and dramatic moments. But some of the richest happiness comes in the form of calm. It comes during a walk alone, a shared silence, a quiet moment of completion. These moments do not shout. They do not flood the nervous system. But they are real. And for those who learn to recognize them, they offer a kind of happiness that does not burn out as quickly.

There is also the fear that if you admit you are happy, it will disappear. This fear is not irrational. People have experienced it before. They say something is going well, and soon after, it falls apart. They express joy, and something interrupts it. Over time, they begin to link happiness with loss. They hold back on naming it, as if protecting it by not speaking it aloud. But fear does not preserve happiness. It dims it. It turns it into something fragile, instead of something that can be lived in.

To build a life where happiness stays longer, you must make room for it. Not by demanding it, but by removing the blocks that push it away. These blocks are not just circumstances. They are beliefs. They are emotional patterns. They are habits of mind. If you are constantly preparing for the worst, constantly distracted, or constantly measuring your experience against others, happiness will feel like a guest who cannot get comfortable.

Building emotional durability requires practice. It means allowing yourself to feel good without shrinking. It means learning to trust stillness. It means allowing quiet joy to count as real. It means noticing when you are too distracted to feel anything and gently returning your attention to the moment. It means becoming the kind of person who does not chase happiness like a prize, but lives in a way that creates the conditions for it to arrive.

And when it does arrive, you let it stay. You do not question whether you deserve it. You do not measure its duration. You do not look over your shoulder waiting for it to end. You let it be what it is, a natural, beautiful part of life that cannot be owned, but can be welcomed.

That is how happiness becomes more durable. Not by forcing it to stay, but by learning how to stop pushing it away.

The Illusion of Arrival

There is a fantasy that lives quietly in the background of many lives. It is not always spoken aloud, but it shapes decisions, motivates sacrifice, and drives people to endure long seasons of difficulty. The fantasy is simple: that one day, you will arrive. You will reach the place where everything makes sense. Where the problems stop. Where you can finally rest. Where the effort becomes worth it. This imagined place is not always physical. It might be a job title, a relationship, a number in the bank account, or a certain level of personal growth. It is the arrival point, and it holds the promise of lasting peace.

But arrival, as most people discover too late, is almost always an illusion. The moment you reach what you thought was the end, you realize it is just another point along the way. The relief is temporary. The clarity is incomplete. The satisfaction fades more quickly than expected. And what remains is a sense of confusion. You did what you were supposed to do. You climbed the ladder, crossed the finish line, and passed the test. So why does it still feel like something is missing?

This is the illusion of arrival, the belief that fulfillment lives at the end of a path, rather than within it. It is the misunderstanding that you are incomplete now, but will be complete later. That your worth is still under construction, but one day it will be finished. This belief creates a subtle form of emotional deferral. You put off contentment, joy, and self-acceptance until you reach that imagined place. And when you get there and nothing changes inside, you begin searching for the next destination.

This pattern often starts early. From childhood, people are told to work toward the next stage. Do well in school to get into a good college. Get into a good college to get a good job. Get a good job to build a good life. But at no point in this process is there a true arrival. The expectations simply shift. The definition of success adjusts. The goal becomes bigger. The bar moves. And so the person keeps striving, believing that arrival is still ahead, just out of reach.

The illusion is strengthened by how society rewards certain outcomes. Graduation ceremonies, job offers, promotions, and awards are treated as turning points. They are framed as the moment when everything changes. But most of the time, the internal change does not match the external event. You walk across a stage or receive a title, and then you return to the same version of yourself. The anxiety, the doubt, the longing, it does not vanish. It waits patiently for the applause to end.

People often feel ashamed to admit this. They do not want to say that their achievements felt hollow. That what they worked for did not feel the way they thought it would. So they pretend. They celebrate externally while feeling nothing internally. They say the right words, wear the right smile, and go through the motions. But deep down, they are grieving the loss of a dream they did not know was false. Not the dream itself, but the emotional certainty it promised.

This can create an identity crisis. If you have defined yourself by the pursuit of a goal, what happens when that goal is reached and it does not deliver what you expected? Who are you without striving? What do you aim for when the finish line keeps moving? Some people double down, they set a new goal and continue chasing. Others withdraw, they feel disillusioned and lose motivation. Both reactions are understandable. Both are responses to the collapse of an illusion.

The most painful version of this illusion occurs when someone gives everything to a goal and it still fails to deliver. An athlete who spends years training for a moment that lasts seconds. A student who sacrifices friendships and sleep for a diploma that leads nowhere. An entrepreneur who builds a business only to feel more anxious than before. These are not failures in the traditional sense. They are emotional miscalculations. The person did not expect the outcome to be perfect. They expected it to feel different. When it does not, they are left with a strange combination of pride and emptiness.

There is nothing wrong with setting goals or working toward dreams. The danger is not in the destination, but in the assumption that it will transform you. That it will erase doubt, quiet insecurity, or permanently elevate your sense of worth. External milestones cannot do internal work. They can provide moments of pride and recognition. They can reflect progress. But they cannot resolve the deeper questions of identity, belonging, or peace.

The illusion of arrival is not just about personal goals. It also exists in relationships. Many people believe that once they find the right person, their life will begin. That love will fix what is broken, complete what is missing, and bring lasting contentment. But relationships, like goals, are not destinations. They are living things, full of complexity and unpredictability. Even the best connection cannot carry the weight of saving someone from themselves.

People also believe in arrival through healing. They think that if they work through their trauma, fix their habits, or gain enough self-awareness, they will no longer feel emotional pain. That growth will make them invulnerable. But growth does not eliminate pain. It changes your relationship with it. Healing does not create a permanent state of joy. It creates a deeper capacity for life in all its forms, including joy, grief, fear, and uncertainty. You do not arrive at peace. You learn how to live with yourself more gently.

This shift in understanding is essential. It allows you to approach life without waiting for it to begin. It frees you from the trap of postponement. You stop saying, "I will be happy when," and start asking, "What can I feel now?" You stop asking the future to rescue you from the present. You begin to see that the present, while imperfect, is where all experience happens. It is the only place where anything real occurs.

Even the language of arrival can be messy. People say they are "on the way," "getting there," or "almost ready." But ready for what? Getting where? These phrases suggest that your life is a rehearsal, that you are always in a state of becoming but never being. They delay self-acceptance. They tell you that who you are now is a draft, not a person. But you are already real. You are already living. This is not the preview. This is the story.

The antidote to the illusion of arrival is not to abandon goals, relationships, or healing. It is to stop giving them mythical power. To stop believing they will save you from the ordinary difficulties of being human. You can still strive, still hope, still build. But you do it knowing that even at the top of the mountain, you will still be you. That the view may be beautiful, but it will not erase the journey it took to get there. And it will not prevent the next climb.

There is a kind of freedom in letting go of arrival. It does not mean you stop moving. It means you stop demanding that movement deliver something it cannot. It means you learn to live in process, rather than holding your breath for completion. It means you let life unfold without requiring it to match a script. That freedom does not come from standing still. It comes from knowing that wherever you are, you are not behind.

One reason the illusion of arrival is so widespread is that it has been mythologized. Nearly every major cultural story has a version of it. The hero returns home. The couple ends up together. The prize is claimed. The music swells, the lights fade, and the story concludes with peace. These endings shape expectations, even when people know they are fictional. The idea of finality is comforting. It suggests that chaos can be resolved, that uncertainty can be erased, that life can be wrapped in a clean arc.

But real life does not offer neat closure. Most events that feel significant are followed by more questions, not fewer. You reach a major milestone, and then you are asked to navigate a new set of expectations. You get what you wanted, and then discover new responsibilities attached to it. Arrival, in the real world, is rarely a point of stillness. It is a pivot. A transition into a new phase, often with its own forms of stress and confusion.

People often underestimate how emotionally complex arrival can be. There is joy, yes, but also a strange kind of grief. The journey is over. The structure of pursuit that once defined you dissolves. The clarity of working toward something is replaced with the ambiguity of holding it. The adrenaline that kept you focused fades, and in its place comes a quiet unease. You may not miss the struggle, but you miss the momentum. You miss the certainty of direction.

That unease leads to a kind of emotional disorientation. You achieved what you were supposed to, yet you feel strangely untethered. The goal was supposed to deliver more than it did, and you begin to question whether something is wrong with you for not feeling more satisfied. This internal contradiction is rarely discussed. People are praised for what they accomplish, but not supported through the emotional aftermath of success. They are expected to be fulfilled, but instead they feel suspended, unable to celebrate fully, but unwilling to admit the letdown.

The illusion persists because few people are honest about what arrival feels like. Those who admit to disappointment are often seen as ungrateful. They are told to focus on how far they have come, to think positively, to remember that others would love to be in their position. But these responses ignore a deeper truth, that disappointment can live alongside gratitude. That you can be proud of what you achieved and still feel uncertain about what it means. These are not contradictory emotions. They are part of the same psychological reality.

This is why some people begin to romanticize the pursuit more than the destination. They look back on the journey with a kind of warmth that the arrival never gave them. The challenges, the effort, the anticipation, those brought focus and clarity. The moment of arrival, by contrast, feels less substantial. It marks an end, but not the kind they expected. The structure collapses. The momentum stops. And they are left with space they do not know how to fill.

Sometimes that space reveals things they were too focused to notice before. Relationships that were neglected. Emotions that were suppressed. Fatigue that was ignored. In the quiet that follows arrival, life rushes back in. And not all of it is pleasant. Many people associate this flood of emotion with failure, when in fact it is simply the reentry into life beyond singular focus. It is not a problem. It is the return of perspective.

That return is uncomfortable because it confronts you with what the goal distracted you from. When you are moving toward something, it is easy to avoid the questions that live beneath the surface. You are too busy. Too focused. Too determined. But when you arrive, the silence reveals them. What do you want now? Who are you without this goal? What does this achievement really mean in the context of your life? These are not easy questions. They require honesty, and in many cases, the willingness to admit that you expected too much from an outcome.

These expectations are often shaped by narratives you absorbed rather than created. Parents, mentors, media, and society at large project images of what success should look like and feel like. You internalize those scripts. You follow them. You imagine the emotional payoff they promise. But once you reach the end, you discover that those narratives are incomplete. They describe the surface, not the depth. They outline a path, but not what it feels like to stand at the end of it.

That realization can be disillusioning, but it can also be liberating. It opens the door to a new kind of motivation, one that is not built on chasing the next emotional peak, but on building a life that feels cohesive even in the absence of peaks. You begin to value consistency, alignment, and rhythm. You begin to see growth not as a ladder but as a landscape, with many paths, some of which do not lead upward but inward.

This shift does not eliminate ambition. It matures it. You can still want things, build things, strive for things. But your expectations are different. You do not expect arrival to change your core experience of being alive. You do not expect it to protect you from restlessness, doubt, or sadness. You expect it to give you information, perspective, maybe some tools, but not transformation. That work belongs to a different process. It happens slowly, often quietly, and usually in the moments you used to rush past.

What replaces the illusion of arrival is something more sustainable. You begin to value presence, not as a buzzword but as a skill. You learn how to participate in your life while it is happening, rather than waiting to look back on it. You let meaning accumulate slowly. You let fulfillment rise from repetition, not revelation. You let the ordinary become enough.

You stop asking when things will begin, and start asking what is already here that you have not yet noticed. You stop imagining arrival as an event and begin treating it as a practice. Every day you arrive in your own life, or you do not. Every day you either touch the moment you are in, or you pass through it without contact. This is what replaces arrival as a destination, presence as a habit.

When that habit becomes consistent, you stop searching for the moment that will complete you. You stop postponing peace. You stop deferring joy. You realize that you were never meant to arrive. You were meant to experience it. And experience does not wait at the end. It meets you here.

Trapped in the Upgrade Loop

Upgrading is no longer a choice. It is a condition of participation. You do not just upgrade your phone. You upgrade your habits, your job title, your online profile, your wardrobe, your personality, your thinking. Every part of your identity becomes subject to an invisible demand for refinement. The world around you suggests that the only alternative to upgrading is irrelevance. And so you comply, often without noticing that the loop was never yours to begin with.

The upgrade loop is marketed as empowerment. Companies claim to be giving you tools to be your best self, live more efficiently, and stay ahead. But beneath this message is something less liberating. You are not being offered improvement. You are being sold instability. The tools change constantly. The expectations shift with every season. The standards are fluid, unreachable, and always slightly out of your grasp. As soon as you adjust, the system updates again. Your progress is never allowed to settle.

This is not accidental. It is design. In the world of consumer psychology, dissatisfaction is profitable. A person who feels content is less likely to spend. A person who questions their value, appearance, productivity, or intelligence is more likely to seek external solutions. Products are rarely sold as luxuries anymore. They are framed as necessities for catching up. If you do not buy the latest version, you are left behind. If you do not adapt to the newest platform, you become invisible. The upgrade loop is not just about growth. It is about survival in a culture engineered to reward the restless.

The digital environment reinforces this every day. Algorithms are built to detect engagement, not depth. They push content that is fast, provocative, and emotionally charged. You are encouraged to stay visible by staying reactive. And visibility becomes a kind of currency, not only in terms of influence, but in terms of perceived legitimacy. If you are not upgrading your thoughts, your opinions, your skills, your aesthetics, you risk fading into the background. This is not natural evolution. It is engineered anxiety.

Even authenticity has been absorbed into the upgrade loop. People are told to "be real," but only in ways that perform well. Vulnerability becomes a trend. Minimalism becomes a brand. Transparency becomes a strategy. The pressure to reinvent yourself does not disappear just because you shift into a different aesthetic. It adapts. It finds new language. You are still being asked to perform transformation, even when the transformation is marketed as simplicity.

This system is powerful because it wears the mask of progress. The idea of becoming better is seductive. It feels intelligent. It feels active. But when progress becomes compulsive, it detaches from purpose. You begin to move forward because stillness feels dangerous. You upgrade not because something is broken, but because the world has convinced you that nothing should stay the same for long. You live in fear of becoming static. But motion is not meaning. Change is not always evolution. Sometimes it is just disorientation wearing the costume of ambition.

The upgrade loop even shapes how people think about time. In earlier generations, stability was seen as success. A consistent career, a home you stayed in, a routine that worked, these were signs of maturity. Now, the message is different. You must always be pivoting. You must show that you are staying relevant, adapting, expanding. If you remain in one place for too long, the assumption is that you are no longer growing. Stillness becomes associated with failure.

This shift has consequences. It fractures attention. It creates emotional fatigue. It turns life into a series of resets rather than a path of accumulation. Each phase becomes disposable. Each version of yourself is treated as temporary. You never fully inhabit anything before discarding it for something that promises better results. But in this cycle, you begin to lose cohesion. Your identity becomes a series of recent updates rather than a rooted narrative.

Worse still, the upgrade loop punishes reflection. To pause and ask, "Why am I doing this?" is seen as falling behind. The system is not built for that question. It is built to keep you moving. To fill every space with the next improvement. To convert even rest into preparation. You do not take a break. You recharge to perform better. You do not reflect on your values. You optimize your mindset. You are never allowed to simply exist. You must always be preparing for the next version of yourself.

Not because it promotes change, but because it distorts your relationship with change. You forget what you actually want. You stop asking whether the upgrade serves your needs. You focus instead on whether it aligns with what others are doing. This creates collective pressure. Everyone is upgrading for fear of being the only one who is not. The loop continues not because it works, but because it is shared. It becomes a form of social self-defense.

The cost of this loop is deeper than exhaustion. It is a loss of intimacy with your own life. When you treat everything as a stepping stone to something better, you rarely feel rooted. You do not stay long enough to build memory. You do not linger long enough to understand. Every experience is evaluated through the lens of what it prepares you for, not what it offers in itself. You become a tourist in your own story, moving quickly, documenting highlights, but never settling into the full depth of a single place.

Eventually, this mindset spreads into how you treat people. Relationships become experiences to upgrade, not commitments to grow within. You look for emotional efficiency. You expect fast results. You evaluate others by how well they meet your changing standards, forgetting that depth requires continuity. You begin to fear the ordinary. You forget that the best relationships are not always the most stimulating, but often the most stable. The upgrade loop teaches you to discard, but not how to stay.

To exit the loop, you have to confront the idea that enough is not a failure. That staying the same, for a time, is not laziness. That building slowly is not backward. This requires a different definition of growth, one that values integration over disruption, rhythm over reaction, and consistency over spectacle. It requires the courage to stop moving long enough to ask whether you are still going in a direction that matters.

You can still evolve. You can still improve. But not everything in your life needs to be better. Some things need to be held. Protected. Revisited, not redesigned. You do not have to upgrade everything you touch. You are allowed to let things stay as they are, even if they are no longer the most efficient or fashionable version. The question is not whether it can be improved, but whether the improvement is necessary.

When you stop upgrading for its own sake, you may begin to feel something unfamiliar, stability that is not boring, identity that is not for display, and progress that is not urgent. You begin to feel ownership over your life, not because it is perfect, but because it is chosen. You begin to stay.

There is a subtle but profound shift that happens when you stop upgrading. Time slows down. Not because your life becomes dull, but because it becomes real. You begin to notice details you once moved too quickly to see. The sound of your own thoughts without input. The rhythm of a morning that is not designed for productivity. The texture of conversation that is not meant to be recorded or shared. These moments are not flashy. They do not signal growth to anyone else. But they reveal to you what growth actually feels like, quiet, steady, and grounded.

In this stillness, you also begin to separate desire from distortion. You realize how much of what you once wanted was inherited. Not from your deepest self, but from advertising, algorithms, and social mimicry. You were taught to want certain things because wanting them made you predictable, measurable, and profitable. You were rewarded for those wants with affirmation, likes, discounts, and approval. But when you step outside the loop, those rewards lose their meaning. You begin to crave alignment, not applause. Simplicity, not novelty.

That shift threatens the system. A person who knows what they actually want is hard to sell to. They are not chasing the next fix. They are not susceptible to comparison. They do not need the upgrade to feel valid. This is not just personal liberation. It is economic resistance. The engine of consumer capitalism depends on your insecurity. When you reject the loop, you disrupt the cycle. Not just for yourself, but for everyone who watches you step away and realizes they could do the same.

You also begin to see that permanence is not the enemy. In a world that glorifies change, staying can feel radical. Committing to a path, a place, a person, or a belief system in a time of constant flux takes courage. It means enduring the discomfort of boredom, the tension of doubt, the reality of imperfection. But it also allows for depth. Roots take time. Trust takes repetition. Mastery takes monotony. None of these things fit well into a culture obsessed with reinvention. But they are the things that build a life with weight.

There is a kind of peace that only emerges after you stop upgrading. Not because you have everything figured out, but because you no longer feel the need to fix what was never broken. You look at your routines, and instead of asking how to optimize them, you ask whether they nourish you. You look at your relationships, and instead of wondering how they reflect on your identity, you ask how they shape your character. You look at your body, and instead of wishing it were different, you thank it for carrying you this far.

None of this means you reject progress. It means you begin to define it for yourself. You stop measuring growth by how quickly you change. You start measuring it by how deeply you understand what stays the same. You begin to see growth not as a race toward the future, but as a return to integrity. You stop looking forward for the next version of yourself. You start looking inward for the version that has been waiting to be heard.

This return is not dramatic. It is subtle. It is not announced with a rebrand or an announcement. It happens quietly, in the small decisions you make each day. You choose to keep the old phone because it still works. You wear the same jacket because it feels right. You stay in the relationship because it brings you peace. You keep the job because it gives you time for your family. These choices do not signal ambition to the outside world. But they signal something deeper to you, that your life is not a product to be constantly upgraded, but a home to be lived in.

When that becomes your orientation, the upgrade loop loses its grip. You see it for what it is, a system built to keep you moving so fast you never have time to ask where you are going. A cycle designed to make you feel like you are never enough, so you keep spending, striving, shifting. When you break that pattern, even in small ways, you begin to reclaim a sense of authorship. You begin to write your own definitions. You stop performing transformation and start living truth.

There is no final version of you waiting at the end of the upgrade cycle. There is only the person you already are, waiting for permission to stop running. Not because you have given up, but because you have finally arrived. Not because you found perfection, but because you discovered presence. Not because you became the best version of yourself, but because you made peace with the version who is here now.

It is the understanding that you do not need to earn your right to exist. You do not need to become more valuable to deserve rest. You do not need to be impressive to be worthy of attention. You can live in the body, the rhythm, the identity you already have. And from that place, you can grow in a way that does not fracture you, but heals you. In a way that does not impress the world, but anchors you to it.

The paradox of the upgrade loop is that it promises transformation but delivers fragmentation. It promises progress but breeds instability. It promises freedom but creates dependency. The more you chase the next version of yourself, the further you drift from the person who is capable of choosing wisely in the first place. You become so focused on keeping up that you forget what you were trying to build. And often, what you were trying to build was already good enough.

To escape the loop, you do not need to make a grand declaration. You need only to stop. To notice what you already have. To ask what is truly yours, not what was suggested. To protect what gives your life rhythm. To stay where meaning has already begun to grow. This is not resistance for its own sake. It is resistance for the sake of wholeness.

Because sometimes the bravest thing you can do in a world obsessed with next is to remain fully here.

The safety that makes you unsafe

The Shield That Shatters

A shield is meant to protect. That is its most fundamental purpose, to stand between you and harm. In myth, in war, in technology, the shield represents safety, stability, and control. But protection is not inherently safe. A shield, if too rigid or too confident in its power, can become a trap. It can give the illusion of invulnerability while hiding the truth: that defense, when pushed to an extreme, becomes fragility. This is the paradox. What protects you in the short term can expose you in the long term. The stronger the shield, the more catastrophic its failure.

In the modern world, this paradox reveals itself not just in physical combat, but across systems, economies, technologies, and infrastructures. The shield is no longer just a metal plate or a concrete bunker. It is a cybersecurity firewall, a geopolitical defense doctrine, an insurance-backed economy, or an algorithm trained to suppress risk. Each one promises safety. Each one, when overused or overtrusted, creates new layers of vulnerability that did not exist before. The very act of shielding, when misapplied, becomes an accelerant to the danger it tries to avoid.

One of the clearest illustrations of this is found in the world of cybersecurity. As digital threats evolved, organizations created increasingly sophisticated systems to guard against intrusion. Firewalls, encryption layers, access controls, behavioral monitoring, the modern cybersecurity stack resembles an impenetrable fortress. And yet, breaches still happen. In fact, some of the worst breaches have occurred in highly protected environments. Why? Because complexity becomes its own kind of exposure. When systems are so layered and intricate that only a few people understand them, a single flaw can ripple invisibly across the whole structure. The shield, once a strength, becomes a blind spot.

It is not just the presence of the shield, but the belief in it, that creates danger. Systems that appear secure often lead people to act with more carelessness. This is known as the Peltzman effect, a principle from risk compensation theory. When drivers were first given seatbelts, studies showed that they drove faster and more aggressively. The safety device gave them confidence, but that confidence led to more risky behavior. The shield improved survival rates in crashes, but it did not reduce crashes themselves. This same principle echoes in software design, investment strategy, and even military doctrine. The more protected you feel, the more likely you are to flirt with risk.

In war, shields have evolved into doctrines of deterrence. The most infamous is nuclear mutually assured destruction, the idea that no country will attack if every country can annihilate each other. This form of shielding has worked, in a narrow sense, to prevent full-scale global war. But it has also led to escalation, secrecy, and a new class of existential risk. Instead of building peace, the shield has institutionalized fear. It requires constant readiness for catastrophe, endless upgrades, and blind faith in systems that must never fail. The defense itself becomes the threat.

What is often forgotten is that every shield is a static object in a dynamic world. It is built to block a specific kind of force, under specific conditions. But the world does not hold still. Threats evolve. Environments shift. Opponents adapt. A shield that once worked can become obsolete in months, or even days, if the conditions change. And often, the shield delays this realization. It allows systems to feel safe even as the ground beneath them rots. The belief in protection becomes more dangerous than the threat it was built to resist.

Nowhere is this more visible than in the architecture of financial risk. Before the 2008 financial crisis, banks and investors believed they had engineered the perfect shields, credit default swaps, risk tranching, stress tests, regulatory buffers. The models said everything was fine. The systems were diversified, the institutions were capitalized, the math was sound. But the shield had cracks. No one noticed because everyone trusted the shield. When it failed, the collapse was deeper because the exposure had been hidden. Risk had not been eliminated. It had been disguised, packaged, and multiplied.

This is the paradox of modern safety systems. They do not always reduce risk. They redistribute it. They make it harder to see, harder to feel, and easier to ignore until it becomes catastrophic. These are not shields. They are delay mechanisms. They buy time, and in doing so, create an illusion of control. But when the time runs out, the impact is greater than if no shield had been there at all. The systems absorb pressure until they can no longer hold it. And when they break, they do not bend. They shatter.

The natural world offers a sobering parallel. Forests that are aggressively protected from fire develop dangerous accumulations of dead wood and underbrush. Over time, the lack of small, natural fires leads to an overload of fuel. When a fire finally does break out, and it always does, it is uncontrollable. The shield, in this case, is fire suppression policy. Intended to protect, it creates the conditions for catastrophe. Ecosystems that evolved with fire as a renewal mechanism are destabilized when the shield prevents the very events they need to survive.

This is not an argument against protection. It is a warning against absolutism. The shield that never adapts becomes a risk in itself. The shield that encourages overconfidence distorts reality. The shield that prevents all stress weakens the structure it guards. Real safety requires feedback, not just force. It requires transparency, not just complexity. It requires that we understand the limits of protection, not just what it defends against, but what it enables by being there.

In many systems, what begins as a shield ends up creating an arms race. Cybersecurity leads to more sophisticated hacking. Police armor leads to more militarized weapons on the street. Encrypted communications lead to more advanced surveillance techniques. Each innovation in defense creates a response in offense, which then prompts new layers of defense. The cycle is infinite. It escalates not toward peace, but toward complexity, fragility, and paranoia. And at every level, participants believe they are only protecting themselves.

This illusion is compounded by the fact that effective shields rarely get credit. When a defense system works, nothing happens. There is no visible crisis. No headlines. No feedback. This encourages a kind of drift, budget cuts, relaxed standards, complacency. The shield is taken for granted. Or worse, it is dismantled precisely because it worked too well. In such cases, safety becomes its own undoing. The lack of visible threat creates an opening for the threat to return stronger.

The most dangerous shields are the ones that are invisible. These are the assumptions, narratives, and cultural myths that shape how institutions operate. A belief in technological superiority. A sense of national exceptionalism. A faith in infinite growth. These mental shields protect identity, pride, and legacy, but they also blind leaders to change. When a country believes it is immune to collapse, it ignores the early signs of decline. When a company believes its brand is invincible, it stops innovating. The shield becomes delusion.

In some cases, the very act of shielding creates a new form of dependency. Take predictive algorithms in financial trading or healthcare diagnostics. These systems are designed to detect problems before they emerge. They are meant to guard against failure. But they also shift agency. Decisions are deferred to models. Human judgment is diminished. When the models fail — as they eventually do — the damage is amplified by the fact that no one knows how to act without them. The shield does not just fail. It paralyzes the system when it does.

This is not a call to abandon protection. Humans need shields. Societies need defense. But we must design shields with the awareness that they are temporary, situational, and fallible. They must be audited, challenged, and updated constantly. More importantly, we must never confuse the presence of a shield with the absence of danger. Safety is not a state. It is a dynamic relationship between exposure and adaptation. And a good shield does not prevent all harm. It allows for just enough stress to keep the system honest.

Resilience does not come from never being hit. It comes from knowing how to recover. A shield that breaks cleanly and predictably is better than one that hides damage until it explodes. In this way, the most dangerous shield is not the one that is weak. It is the one that appears too strong to fail. That illusion of permanence makes it hard to question, hard to test, and impossible to replace. By the time it breaks, it is already too late.

The modern world is full of these brittle protections. Too big to fail banks. Infallible AI systems. Military deterrence doctrines. Infrastructure rated for last century's weather. Each is built with the assumption that the worst will not happen, or if it does, the shield will hold. But history suggests otherwise. The Titanic. Chernobyl. Fukushima. The 2008 crash. Each case involved a protective system that failed not just in design, but in imagination. The shield shattered because no one believed it could.

The solution is not to abandon defense, but to reimagine it. To build shields that are transparent, flexible, and open to challenge. To reward systems that surface near-failures instead of hiding them. To teach people that safety is not the absence of vulnerability, but the ability to respond to it. And to remember that the best shields do not just block harm. They help you see the danger before it arrives.

The shield that shatters is not just a failure of material. It is a failure of mindset. It is the belief that safety can be permanent, that complexity guarantees control, that the presence of defense equals the absence of risk. Real strength is not found in what you block. It is found in how you adapt when the shield gives way.

Because eventually, it always does

To understand how dangerous protective systems can become when stretched beyond their limits, we must look beyond individual failures and examine patterns, not just of materials or policies, but of belief. Belief in the strength of a system is often what makes it fragile. This is a paradox that exists not just in infrastructure, but in institutions, ideologies, and even science.

Consider the history of cryptography. For decades, encryption standards were treated as unbreakable shields. The confidence in those systems allowed critical infrastructure, banking systems, and government communication to rely on them entirely. But every shield has a lifespan. With the emergence of quantum computing, many of those once impervious codes are now considered vulnerable. The assumption that a protective system can stand forever, simply because it has not yet failed, blinds people to the reality that change is inevitable, and failure is not a matter of if, but when. A shield that is not designed to evolve is already in the process of breaking.

The danger here is not in the encryption itself. The danger is in the systemic overconfidence it fosters. When an entire society believes a shield will always work, it builds dependencies around that assumption. It allows essential systems to lean harder on the very thing that may soon give out. This creates a single point of catastrophic failure, made worse by the fact that no one prepared for it. Safety becomes the most fragile belief a society can hold.

Even nature carries lessons about how protective strategies can turn to risk. Take the behavior of certain animals in the wild. Many prey species have evolved intricate defense mechanisms, including camouflage, toxic chemicals, and hard shells. These protections work well when predators behave predictably. But when environments change rapidly, or predators evolve faster, the shield becomes ineffective. Worse, some species become so specialized in their defense that they cannot adapt quickly enough when new threats appear. The defense that once preserved them now traps them in extinction. Evolution punishes rigidity, even if it once offered protection.

This lesson applies just as strongly to systems built by humans. Organizations that rely too heavily on legacy protocols, outdated procedures, or historical assumptions often find themselves unable to respond to disruption. Their structures are optimized for protection, not for adaptation. Like a medieval fortress in an era of drones, they are fortified in the wrong ways. The result is not resilience, but exposure, vulnerability disguised as strength.

We see similar effects in complex bureaucracies. When a problem arises, the instinct is often to build a new protocol, department, or oversight committee to prevent it from happening again. Each of these is a kind of shield, a mechanism to reduce blame, delay risk, or compartmentalize failure. But over time, the accumulation of these shields becomes a burden. The system grows heavy, inflexible, and unable to respond to new challenges. By trying to protect itself from every possible danger, it becomes incapable of handling the one that finally arrives. The shield that was meant to prevent collapse becomes the very cause of collapse.

This failure of structure is mirrored in artificial intelligence and automation. As more decision making is handed over to complex models and predictive algorithms, institutions begin to treat those tools as infallible. These systems are designed to prevent error, bias, and inefficiency. But they also create new kinds of opacity. The reasoning behind decisions becomes harder to trace. Failures become harder to diagnose. When the algorithm makes a mistake, no one knows who is responsible. The shield absorbs accountability, but it also erases it. Protection at that scale does not just prevent harm. It prevents understanding.

These shields do not collapse slowly. They collapse all at once. The longer they are trusted without examination, the more pressure they absorb. And the more pressure they absorb, the more catastrophic their failure. This is the danger of untested strength, the kind that looks invincible because it has never been put under real stress.

One of the most overlooked examples of this is in international treaties and global agreements. These are designed to be diplomatic shields, frameworks that prevent conflict, enforce cooperation, and maintain stability. But treaties that are too rigid, too idealistic, or too difficult to amend can create frozen tensions. Countries bound by outdated agreements may face evolving threats that the original terms never anticipated. When those pressures build and the treaty no longer serves reality, it can collapse in crisis. Trust evaporates. Alliances fracture. The illusion of protection makes the rupture even more severe.

Even in the world of public communication, protective strategies can backfire. Governments often withhold information during crises to prevent panic. This is a kind of shield, protection through controlled narrative. But when the truth inevitably emerges, the trust erodes faster than any misinformation ever could. The shield that was meant to protect public order becomes a symbol of betrayal. It does not matter whether the shield worked in the short term. Its long term collapse damages every institution associated with it.

In all of these examples, the core problem is not the act of shielding itself. It is the refusal to test, question, or evolve the shield. No defense should be permanent. No protective system should be immune from scrutiny. The more sacred a shield becomes, the more dangerous it is. This is where the paradox becomes clearest. True safety requires a willingness to expose the shield to damage. If you cannot examine it, adjust it, or admit its weaknesses, it becomes a liability. The strongest shields are not the ones that never break. They are the ones that break in predictable, controlled ways and then get rebuilt.

Engineers understand this principle deeply. Buildings in earthquake zones are not designed to be rigid. They are designed to sway. The flexibility prevents collapse. Rigid structures, no matter how strong they seem, are more likely to snap under extreme stress. This is the difference between protection and resilience. One resists damage. The other absorbs it and recovers. The best shield is not the one that stops the earthquake. It is the one that lets the building survive it.

In the realm of public health, we can see how this principle plays out in vaccination strategies. The idea of herd immunity is a kind of population level shield. But it only works if the protection is dynamic, updated to match mutations, distributed equitably, and supported by transparent communication. When the shield becomes politicized, or when it is assumed to be a permanent fix, it collapses in trust. People begin to reject it, not because they are irrational, but because the shield has not evolved with their concerns. Protection cannot be imposed. It must be earned, rebuilt, and responsive to new threats.

The danger of the shield is that it hides these dynamics. It makes people feel protected even when the conditions have changed. It delays confrontation. It encourages dependency. And when it fails, it fails harder than expected, because no one imagined that it could.

This is the deepest paradox of all. The shield that protects you in the short term increases your exposure in the long term, not just because of what it fails to stop, but because of how it reshapes your behavior, your systems, and your sense of what is safe.

To live well in a world of uncertainty, we must learn to distinguish between temporary defenses and permanent illusions. We must design shields that are open to critique, failure, and renewal. We must build systems that are not just strong, but also soft in the right places, capable of yielding without collapsing.

And above all, we must never confuse the absence of disaster with the presence of safety. Because sometimes, the most dangerous moment is the one when the shield is still holding, and no one is looking underneath it.

The Fragility of Overprotection

Protection is a natural instinct. From the moment we are born, our environments are shaped by the efforts of others to shield us from harm. Walls are built, rules are enforced, and routines are created to ensure our safety. In families, in schools, in cities, and in global policies, protection is a constant design goal. But protection, like any force taken to an extreme, begins to bend back on itself. It no longer preserves strength. It begins to suppress it. When protection becomes overprotection, what was once a buffer turns into a brittle shell. And this is the paradox, the more a system is insulated from harm, the less it learns how to handle harm. What is safe in the moment becomes unsafe over time.

To understand this, we must think about how strength is actually built. In biology, muscles grow when they are stressed. A small amount of damage triggers repair and growth. Bones become denser when exposed to resistance. Even the immune system learns through exposure to pathogens. Every durable structure in nature develops through a process of controlled failure. It is not the avoidance of harm that builds strength. It is the capacity to recover from it. When this process is blocked, the system loses its resilience. It may look stable, but it is not prepared for shock.

This idea plays out across all scales of human life. In parenting, for example, overprotection often stems from love and fear. A parent who shields a child from every failure, every mistake, every frustration, may feel they are acting in the child's best interest. But what they are doing, often unintentionally, is interrupting the child's ability to learn discomfort. A child who never hears the word no becomes confused by the first rejection they face. A child who never climbs and falls never learns how to navigate risk. Overprotection creates fragility not by harming, but by removing the very discomforts that teach recovery.

This is not limited to childhood. Educational institutions often create tightly controlled environments that reward compliance and discourage uncertainty. Students are given safe tasks, clear grading rubrics, and predictable outcomes. But when they step outside into the real world, they are suddenly expected to handle ambiguity, failure, and contradiction — experiences they were never prepared for. The institutions protected them too well, and in doing so, left them vulnerable to everything that falls outside the scripted environment. Overprotection in learning leads to brittle intelligence, knowledge that cracks when it is no longer contained.

In a similar way, companies that grow under sheltered conditions often falter when exposed to real competition. A startup that survives only through subsidies, inflated valuations, or artificial demand may appear successful, but the moment market forces shift, it collapses. The business was protected from natural stressors. It never learned to adapt. Overprotection creates a sense of stability, but that stability is only as deep as the next disruption. When the environment changes, and it always does, the untested system fails.

We can also observe this in economic systems that cushion every dip in the market. Governments and central banks, out of fear of recession, often inject liquidity or cut interest rates at the first sign of volatility. These interventions may calm markets in the short term, but over time, they reduce the system's ability to self correct. Investors become dependent on bailouts. Corporations take greater risks, expecting rescue. The market, once a living system of checks and balances, becomes a fragile structure propped up by continuous intervention. Overprotection here does not eliminate risk. It moves it, hides it, and magnifies it.

This fragility is particularly dangerous because it is not always visible. In fact, overprotected systems often look calm, polished, and efficient. A smooth surface is mistaken for durability. But just as glass can look flawless while being one crack away from shattering, an overprotected society can seem stable until a single shock reveals its weakness. A transportation grid that never faces winter storms may crumble during one. A digital infrastructure that never trains for outages may collapse under a power surge. A healthcare system that is protected from patient surges may implode during a pandemic. The calm hides the cost.

Part of what makes overprotection so appealing is the illusion of control. It is comforting to believe that risk can be engineered away, that if we build the right systems, follow the right rules, and add enough safety measures, nothing will go wrong. But this belief ignores a fundamental truth about reality, no system can be fully isolated from stress. And when you try to eliminate every possible source of harm, you often eliminate the very conditions that build tolerance.

Take fire suppression, for instance. In forests that are aggressively protected from small, natural fires, dead material builds up. Over years, this accumulation creates a massive fuel load. When a fire eventually breaks out, and it always does, it becomes uncontrollable. What would have been a small cleansing event becomes a catastrophic blaze. The overprotection was not neutral. It stored up risk. And when the risk finally emerged, it did so with amplified force.

There is also a psychological dimension to this paradox. Individuals raised in highly protective environments often experience anxiety when faced with uncertainty. Not because they are weaker by nature, but because they have never been trained in emotional discomfort. They were protected from distress instead of taught how to navigate it. The absence of adversity does not create peace. It creates fear of the unknown. Overprotection robs people of their ability to interpret stress as something survivable. Every problem becomes a threat. Every setback becomes a crisis. Fragility becomes a mindset.

In international development, this paradox plays out in how aid is structured. In some regions, continuous flows of external assistance have created dependencies. Communities stop building their own resilience because the safety net is always there. When that support is withdrawn or delayed, the systems collapse. The aid was not malicious, but it created a false equilibrium — one in which local structures never had to build strength through adversity. Over time, generosity replaced strategy, and fragility took root beneath the surface.

Even in technology, we can see how overprotection leads to brittle systems. Consider software designed with too many guardrails. Every user decision is blocked by warnings, confirmations, and safety prompts. The result is a slower experience, and worse, an overreliance on the system to think for the user. When something goes wrong, a glitch, a corrupted file, an unexpected input, the user is unprepared to troubleshoot. The system was so protective that it created helplessness. When the safety net fails, the user has no tools left.

This pattern shows up again and again, because the logic of overprotection is wanted. It promises peace, predictability, and stability. But it delivers the opposite when the world shifts. A system that never experiences strain cannot grow stronger. It simply grows more fragile in secret. The longer it is protected, the more spectacular its collapse becomes.

There is a concept in systems thinking called antifragility. It refers to the opposite of fragility, not robustness, but improvement through stress. An antifragile system benefits from variability. It grows stronger with volatility, pressure, and even small failures. This is what overprotection prevents. By shielding a system from stress, you remove the very conditions that would allow it to evolve. Overprotection is not just fragility. It is the prevention of growth.

We must be careful, then, about how we define success in protected environments. A child who never fails is not thriving. A market that never dips is not healthy. A nation that never changes is not stable. Strength cannot be measured by the absence of pain. It must be measured by the presence of resilience, the ability to bend, adapt, and come back stronger. Overprotection removes that ability.

To resist this paradox, we must design systems that include controlled stress. We must allow for error, discomfort, and feedback. We must build schools that teach through challenges, workplaces that tolerate smart failure, and cities that learn through stress tests. Protection is not the enemy, but it must be a gateway, not a cage. It must serve development, not delay it.

And perhaps most of all, we must challenge the mindset that safety means the absence of risk. True safety is not the suppression of difficulty. It is the capacity to navigate it. Fragility is not created by stress. It is created by the absence of stress for too long.

One of the most vivid illustrations of overprotection's fragility can be found in the way modern cities are planned and maintained. In many developed countries, urban environments are obsessively engineered to remove all possible inconveniences. Potholes are patched immediately, sidewalks are leveled, traffic patterns are controlled by sophisticated systems, and even lighting is optimized for safety and comfort. But while this design may seem ideal, it creates an environment in which people lose their natural attentiveness. Pedestrians stop looking down. Drivers rely too heavily on navigation. Cyclists assume that all paths are smooth. Then, when a system fails, a power outage disables the traffic lights, a cracked sidewalk causes a trip, a detour removes the expected route, accidents spike. People are no longer calibrated to unpredictability. The infrastructure may be pristine, but the people using it have lost their adaptability. Safety was maximized, but awareness was minimized.

In rural environments, by contrast, people often operate under more unpredictable conditions. Roads may be unpaved. Directions may be unclear. Emergencies may need personal solutions. While these environments come with their own risks, they also build a kind of resilience that urban design suppresses. The individual becomes more attentive, more resourceful, and more aware of their surroundings. In the long term, overprotection makes cities fragile in a different way, not because of the design itself, but because of how it shapes human behavior within it. It teaches people to assume safety is a constant. And when that illusion breaks, they are unprepared.

This same dynamic appears in digital safety. Consider password managers, biometric authentication, and seamless logins. These tools are designed to reduce friction and improve security, but they also encourage users to disengage from their own protection. People forget their actual passwords. They lose the ability to manually log in. When a failure occurs, a server outage, a hacked system, or a lost device, they cannot access anything without the tool they relied on. The overprotection did not just hide the complexity. It removed the user's readiness. In the pursuit of frictionless security, the result was helplessness.

In geopolitical terms, overprotection manifests in how some nations build military alliances. A country that relies too heavily on the presence of a powerful ally may reduce its own investment in defense. It may allow its training, infrastructure, and preparedness to degrade, assuming that external forces will step in during a crisis. But when those alliances are strained, delayed, or withdrawn, the dependent nation finds itself exposed. Overprotection in this context creates a false sense of invulnerability. The shield feels permanent, but it was never designed to be the only defense. Fragility here is not military weakness. It is a strategic assumption.

This is not to say that protection should be abandoned. Rather, the problem lies in the absence of calibration. Systems need stress to improve, but the stress must be proportional and intentional. Children need to fail safely. Markets need to fluctuate within boundaries. Technologies need users who understand their inner workings. Societies need discomfort to evolve. Overprotection removes these gradients. It replaces dynamic learning with passive trust. And trust, when misplaced, leads to collapse.

In the workplace, we also see the damage overprotection can cause. Managers who avoid difficult conversations to protect morale often create toxic silence. Employees begin to fear feedback instead of learning from it. Small problems fester into large ones. Teams become fragile, unable to adapt to changing demands or address internal conflicts. A leader may think they are shielding their team, but they are actually creating a culture where discomfort is equated with danger. Growth stalls. Innovation suffers. And when pressure increases, whether from deadlines, turnover, or competition, the team breaks down. What looked like harmony was actually avoidance.

Another overlooked area where overprotection shows its cracks is in mental health. Societies that promote constant comfort, instant gratification, and emotional shielding often see rising rates of anxiety and depression. It is not because comfort itself is harmful, but because it becomes the only standard. People are taught to avoid pain at all costs. Difficult conversations, setbacks, boredom, and even solitude are treated as things to be medicated, reframed, or avoided altogether. But a healthy mind is one that can endure discomfort without breaking. Overprotection creates the opposite, a psychological structure that is fine as long as nothing goes wrong.

When it does, the person spirals, not because they are weak, but because they were never taught how to navigate pain.

This fragility becomes generational. Children raised without the space to be uncomfortable often become adults who cannot tolerate ambiguity. They fear change, avoid confrontation, and seek environments where everything is predictable. This can lead to political extremism, cultural rigidity, and even economic paralysis. People cling to systems that no longer serve them simply because they are familiar. The fear of discomfort becomes stronger than the desire for progress. At scale, this is not just an individual problem. It becomes a societal crisis. Progress halts. Institutions calcify. And when external pressure arrives, the entire structure collapses under the weight of its own artificial peace.

One of the clearest metaphors for this is the greenhouse. Plants raised in a greenhouse are protected from wind, drought, pests, and extreme temperatures. They thrive under perfect conditions. But the moment they are transplanted outside, they struggle. Their roots are shallow. Their leaves are weak. Their internal chemistry is not prepared for variability. The greenhouse created beauty, but not strength. This is what overprotection does. It crafts ideal conditions that are disconnected from the real world. The result is something that looks healthy until reality arrives.

To resist this, designers, leaders, and individuals must learn to build friction back into the system. Not as punishment, but as preparation. Educational systems should allow for failure. Medical systems should prepare for overload. Economic policies should assume fluctuation. Parents should let their children face setbacks. Communities should allow disagreement. And people, above all, should become comfortable with the fact that strength does not come from control. It comes from exposure, recovery, and continuous adaptation.

Protection is important. But when it becomes excessive, it stops being a service and becomes a sedative. It convinces us that we are safe when we are merely numb. It delays the crisis instead of preventing it. And it makes every future challenge more severe by robbing us of the chance to rehearse it in smaller ways.

The fragility of overprotection lies in this simple truth — if you are always safe, you never learn how to be strong. And if you never learn how to be strong, the first real threat is always the hardest one.

When Precaution Becomes the Threat

Precaution is supposed to be a virtue. It reflects foresight, responsibility, and rational thinking. It is what keeps planes from crashing, bridges from collapsing, and economies from spiraling into chaos. It is the logic behind safety nets, disaster drills, emergency savings, and regulatory oversight. But like every other system rooted in protection, precaution becomes dangerous when it grows unchecked. At some point, caution crosses a line and becomes its own form of risk. It begins to interfere with the very resilience it was designed to preserve. The act of shielding against one danger quietly invites another, often more subtle and destructive.

This paradox has always existed, but it becomes particularly sharp in modern systems, where the speed of decision making and the scale of consequences are both higher than ever. The challenge is not in deciding whether to be cautious or reckless. It is in recognizing when precaution has shifted from prevention to paralysis, from planning to fear, from wisdom to avoidance.

We begin to see this in the way institutions approach regulation. Consider the financial industry after a major market crash. In response to volatility, governments and agencies often introduce sweeping new restrictions. These are designed to prevent repetition of the crisis, to lock down risk, and to make the system safer. But each regulation adds a layer of complexity. It makes compliance more expensive, more technical, and often more abstract. Over time, smaller players are pushed out of the market. Innovation is slowed, not because new ideas are worse, but because the cost of precaution makes experimentation nearly impossible.

Worse, in some cases, the new regulations do not address the real source of the previous crisis. They are reactionary, based on past events rather than future vulnerabilities. This misalignment creates a false sense of security. Institutions feel protected because the rules are tighter, but those rules may be guarding against threats that no longer exist while ignoring new ones. The precaution, then, becomes the threat. It makes the system more fragile by slowing its ability to adapt to reality.

A similar dynamic appears in medicine. Preventive health is often seen as the highest form of care. Catching disease early, modifying risk factors, and encouraging lifestyle changes can save lives. But the line between prevention and overdiagnosis is thin. When systems become obsessed with catching every possible illness, they begin to treat the healthy as sick. People are subjected to unnecessary scans, tests, and medications. The anxiety of disease replaces the reality of health. Patients become dependent on surveillance. False positives lead to harmful treatments. The medical system, in trying to prevent suffering, creates it.

This is not a failure of science. It is a misapplication of precaution. It assumes that more data, more scanning, and more preemptive action always lead to better outcomes. But the human body is complex, and not every abnormality is a threat. Not every variation is a signal of collapse. In trying to stop every possibility of harm, the system harms through excess. The precaution causes stress, fear, and sometimes irreversible interventions. The body is treated not as a living system with fluctuations, but as a machine that must be constantly monitored and tuned. This mindset robs individuals of peace, and more importantly, it distracts practitioners from genuine threats that deserve attention.

In the world of infrastructure, precaution often comes in the form of redundancy. Backup systems are installed. Emergency protocols are rehearsed. But when every failure is anticipated and every system is doubled, something subtle happens. Operators begin to rely on the backups. They become complacent. The assumption is that if anything goes wrong, there is another system in place to catch it. This creates a dangerous dependency. The original systems are maintained with less care. The human vigilance that once kept errors in check fades. And when the backup fails, and eventually it will, the entire structure collapses because no one was paying attention.

This is known in engineering as risk compensation. The more safety features a system includes, the more people tend to behave carelessly. A driver in a car with advanced brakes, lane assistance, and airbags may drive more aggressively. A climber using superior harnesses may take routes beyond their skill. The precaution enables riskier behavior. What was intended as protection becomes a reason to push the limit. And when the limit is reached, the damage is worse than it would have been without the extra safety features.

At the societal level, we see precaution turning into threat through the politics of fear. After a major crisis, whether a terrorist attack, a pandemic, or a cyber incident, governments often respond by expanding surveillance, restricting mobility, and centralizing power. These actions are framed as temporary, necessary, and precautionary. But history shows that many of these measures become permanent. They outlast the crisis. They reshape civil liberties. And over time, they change the relationship between citizens and authority.

The justification is always safety. But what begins as a protective measure slowly becomes a tool of control. A population conditioned to accept precautionary overreach loses its ability to resist intrusion. It trades freedom for the illusion of protection. And in doing so, it becomes less safe, not more. The threat is no longer external. It is embedded in the system itself.

We can also observe this paradox in environmental policy. In an effort to prevent ecological damage, some governments impose strict regulations on land use, development, and resource extraction. These are important and often necessary. But when taken too far, or applied without nuance, they can create unintended damage. For example, preventing all logging in a fire-prone forest may increase the risk of uncontrollable wildfires, as dead material builds up without natural thinning. Restricting all human intervention in certain ecosystems may allow invasive species to flourish unchecked. The goal of precaution becomes a refusal to intervene, and that refusal creates its own form of collapse.

Precaution, when rigid, does not always protect the system. Sometimes it freezes it in place. And systems that cannot move eventually break.

This is especially true in technology and artificial intelligence. In an effort to prevent unethical uses of advanced models, companies and regulators often restrict access, delay innovation, or create heavy oversight frameworks. The intent is noble, to avoid bias, exploitation, and harm. But in doing so, the development shifts to less transparent players, often in environments with lower ethical standards. Open platforms are shut down, while shadow systems grow. The precaution silences the responsible, and empowers the reckless.

This paradox is difficult to resolve because it is rooted in good intentions. No one implements a precautionary policy with the desire to create harm. The harm emerges indirectly, over time, as the policy distorts behavior, discourages adaptation, and erodes individual judgment. It replaces human responsibility with procedural overreach. It turns active agents into passive subjects.

The solution is not to abandon precaution. It is to recognize its limits. Precaution should always be measured against the cost of inaction, the potential for distortion, and the long term adaptability of the system it affects. It should be designed with exit strategies, feedback loops, and mechanisms for revision. A precaution that cannot be questioned is no longer safe. It is dogma.

True resilience does not come from building higher walls. It comes from building smarter gates, systems that allow feedback, that adjust to conditions, and that remain accountable to those they protect. The safest society is not the one with the most precaution. It is the one with the most responsive intelligence.

There is a moment when preparation turns into obsession, when the effort to avoid failure creates a new path toward it. This moment is rarely visible. It does not arrive with noise or headlines. It creeps in through good policy, well-meaning plans, and protective logic. It is not the absence of thought. It is the overapplication of it.

Precaution becomes dangerous when it forgets its place, when it no longer supports action, but replaces it. There is a difference between planning to move and never leaving the starting point. In this gap, the illusion of action can be mistaken for actual progress. Plans are drafted, scenarios are simulated, and alerts are installed. But the problem remains untouched, because the system is now designed to avoid all risk, including the risk of acting too late.

The paralysis begins quietly. It appears as prudence. An extra layer of approval is added. A few more conditions are included. A pause is requested until more information is available. On paper, it looks rational. But underneath, the system is training itself to fear consequences more than it values progress. It becomes more important to avoid a mistake than to solve a problem.

This mindset is particularly dangerous when adopted by leadership. A cautious leader is respected. A paralyzed one creates a culture of avoidance. People stop proposing new solutions because they fear blame. Meetings become rituals of deferral. The language shifts. Instead of asking what should be done, people ask what should be avoided. Instead of identifying opportunity, they begin to list liabilities. This is not a strategy. It is stagnation disguised as responsibility.

Systems designed around excessive precaution develop patterns of retreat. They remove pressure rather than resolve it. When something appears volatile, the instinct is to contain it, silence it, or push it outside the system. But pressure does not disappear. It collects. Avoided conflict becomes resentment. Deferred innovation becomes decay. Ignored inefficiency becomes an embedded cost. The danger is no longer external. It is now structural.

A person who continually defers risk avoids discomfort in the short term, but builds anxiety in the long term. Every decision becomes a potential catastrophe. Every step forward feels like a misstep waiting to happen. Eventually, they stop moving altogether. They mistake fear for wisdom. They believe that because they are anxious, they must be seeing danger more clearly. But in truth, they are seeing only the shadow of danger, magnified, distorted, and pulled across every surface of life.

The brain is not built to calculate endless futures. It can prepare, yes, but it must also act. When precaution becomes an identity, the person is no longer thinking. They are rehearsing a collapse. And rehearsal, without a final act, becomes the act itself. Life becomes a script of imagined disasters, none of which arrive, but all of which drain the energy to face what is real.

Precaution was meant to give peace of mind. Instead, it replaces peace with planning, presence with projection. The future becomes a trap, a maze of what-ifs with no exit. This is where precaution fails not only as strategy, but as worldview. It feeds the illusion that control can be complete, that all risk is avoidable, that every outcome can be anticipated. It cannot. And in pretending otherwise, the person or system creates fragility in the one place it cannot afford it, the mind.

Even in public decision making, the weight of precaution can lead to injustice. When institutions demand absolute certainty before acting, problems that are real but subtle remain unresolved. A known hazard may be dismissed because it does not reach the threshold of proof. A pattern of harm may be ignored because it is not statistically explosive. The demand for irrefutable evidence delays intervention. The system becomes so afraid of acting prematurely that it chooses not to act at all. And the result is quiet suffering, unseen by headlines, but constant.

Movement with accountability, adjustment, and revision. Systems must not wait until harm is undeniable to begin addressing it. By that point, it is not precaution anymore. It is an apology. And apologies, though necessary, do not repair preventable damage.

To break free from this trap, a different kind of wisdom is required, the wisdom to act without full certainty, the discipline to revise in motion, and the courage to tolerate backlash. A decision made too late may be safer in hindsight, but safety is not the only value. Effectiveness matters. So does integrity. So does urgency.

Precaution should not become the standard of virtue. Nor should it become the weapon of critics who argue that no step should be taken until the outcome is fully known. Life does not allow such guarantees. The most important decisions in history, in science, policy, and personal life, have never been made under perfect clarity. They have always been made with tension, resistance, and risk.

What separates the systems that endure from those that collapse is not how well they avoided error. It is how well they recognized when precaution was no longer serving them. When safety became a disguise for stasis. When fear began to overwrite purpose.

This is the paradox. The desire to do no harm becomes the reason harm is allowed to continue. The system refuses to adapt because adaptation requires risk. But refusing to adapt is the greatest risk of all.

Collapse of care

Care is one of the most powerful forces in a society. At its best, care is what holds people together, lifts them during crisis, and sustains them when systems fail. It is the unspoken current running beneath healthcare, education, governance, and family. But care, like any form of protection, is not immune to distortion. When scaled, systematized, or abstracted, care can lose its soul. It becomes a protocol. It becomes a checkbox. It becomes a service rather than a responsibility. And eventually, in the attempt to provide for everyone, it begins to serve no one. This is the collapse of care, not the disappearance of the structure, but the disappearance of meaning within it.

The collapse does not always look dramatic. Often, it looks like more paperwork, longer wait times, or staff who no longer make eye contact. It looks like a hospital where a patient is treated efficiently but leaves feeling like a number. It looks like a school where grades are given, rules are followed, and yet the students feel unseen. It looks like government programs with rising budgets and falling trust. The structure remains. The intention remains. But something essential has been lost. The care itself is gone.

This paradox is difficult to name because the systems still appear to be working. There are still nurses, still teachers, still counselors, still social workers. There are still safety nets, support lines, and wellness apps. But these tools, when separated from human connection, become hollow. They perform the form of care without the presence of it. They distribute resources without distributing attention. The systems were built to protect. But when scaled too far, they begin to ignore the individual they were meant to serve.

At the root of this collapse is often the obsession with coverage. In trying to reach everyone, the system forgets to fully reach anyone. Care becomes a volume problem. How many patients per hour? How many cases are closed? How many meals are served? But care is not a commodity. It cannot be mass produced without something breaking. And what breaks first is empathy. The provider begins to focus on throughput. The recipient begins to feel like a burden. The interaction becomes transactional, not relational. Even when outcomes are met, dignity is not.

Systems now rely heavily on artificial intelligence, automated messaging, and standardized responses. These tools are efficient.

They reduce cost, increase access, and eliminate delay. But they also remove the moment of human connection, the moment where one person sees another, not as a case, but as a life. When care is delivered through templates, even if those templates are accurate, the recipient often feels alone. They sense that no one is truly listening. And over time, this absence of presence becomes a kind of emotional erosion. The structure of care exists, but its weight has been lost.

The slow erosion of care is often invisible because it hides behind good metrics. When a system is judged by how many people it reaches, how quickly it processes requests, or how cost-effective its delivery becomes, it may look successful on paper. But people do not experience paper. They experience presence. They do not feel efficiency. They feel being heard. And when these deeper human markers are missing, a quiet form of damage begins. It is not catastrophic. It is cumulative.

Insurance systems offer a striking example. In theory, they are a structure of care, a promise that no individual will bear the full weight of misfortune alone. But in practice, they often become machines of deflection. Each claim becomes a negotiation. Each illness becomes a puzzle to justify. Language is optimized for denial, not understanding. Customers must prove that their pain is valid, must defend themselves against suspicion, must wait while decisions are processed by unseen algorithms. The intention to protect becomes a game of delay. The experience is not one of care. It is one of exhaustion.

This breakdown happens slowly. A policy changes here. A new form is introduced there. A more efficient review system is implemented. None of these changes are malicious. They are framed as necessary, even responsible. But together, they create distance, the kind of distance where the person in need is separated from the person who can help. Instead of a hand reaching out, there is a list of conditions. Instead of a voice saying "we will help," there is an email saying "your case is under review." The result is not just frustration. It is alienation.

Nurses, teachers, and social workers often enter their fields with deep conviction. They do not choose these paths for money or convenience. They choose them because they want to help. But over time, the system begins to wear them down. Paperwork expands. Autonomy shrinks. Emotional labor goes unrecognized. Time becomes a scarcity. The very act of caring becomes a liability. The system asks them to be present while robbing them of the space to do so.

Eventually, many burn out. Not because they stopped caring, but because caring was not sustainable. They were asked to give more than they had. The collapse of care, in this context, is not just a breakdown in service. It is a loss of soul. A person who wanted to help is now counting the hours until their shift ends. A teacher who once stayed late to support students now stays silent in meetings. A nurse who used to comfort patients now avoids eye contact. These are not failures of character. They are symptoms of a system that protects its own efficiency more than the people inside it.

When care becomes policy, something is always lost. A rule cannot replace judgment. A form cannot capture empathy. A protocol cannot adapt to nuance. Systems must have structure, but when that structure becomes rigid, care becomes brittle. It can only function within certain parameters. It can only respond to problems that fit the categories it was built for. Anything outside the template is ignored or redirected.

This is how people fall through the cracks. Not because no one wants to help, but because the system no longer knows how. The care was abstracted, split into roles, processes, and requirements. Responsibility is diffused. Everyone is following the procedure, but no one is responsible for the outcome. In this vacuum, the human is lost.

And yet, paradoxically, the system may grow in size during this process. Budgets increase. Staff numbers rise. New programs are launched. From a distance, it looks like care is expanding. But inside, the recipients feel more alone than ever. They are bounced from department to department. They are told they do not qualify. They are asked to wait. Their names are misspelled, their needs misunderstood. The system, while larger, is now less capable. It is like a body that has grown heavier but lost its strength.

The fate that was chosen

The Prophecy That Wrote Itself

There is a quiet power in the things people believe will happen. Sometimes, the expectation itself becomes the force that makes it real. Not because the future was fixed from the start, but because belief shaped the decisions that shaped the outcome. This is the paradox of prophecy, the more certain someone is of what will happen, the more they unknowingly act in ways that help bring it to life.

Throughout history, prophecies have carried an eerie weight. Whether carved into ancient stone, spoken by oracles, or printed in headlines, they tend to draw people in. What makes them so powerful is not their accuracy, but the psychological pull they exert. The human brain is built to seek patterns, to look for meaning, and to prepare for the future. When a prophecy is introduced, it plants a narrative seed. Even when dismissed as myth or exaggeration, it lingers in the background, whispering possibilities. The mind, once exposed to a story of what might be, cannot fully unhear it.

But this is where the paradox emerges. A prophecy is supposed to predict the future, yet it often creates it. People do not merely anticipate the outcome, they begin living in response to it. Actions that might not have happened otherwise are taken as a result of trying to prepare, prevent, or pursue what was foretold. In trying to resist the prophecy, they validate it. In trying to fulfill it, they erase any alternative. This is not magic. It is human psychology, played out through behavior and cause and effect.

Consider a CEO who hears a rumor that a recession is coming. No hard data, just early whispers. Nervous, he cuts spending, freezes hiring, and delays investment. His competitors do the same. Consumers notice job slowdowns and begin to save more and spend less. The reduced spending triggers a drop in revenue across industries. The market tightens. The prophecy of recession, once only a suggestion, has been fulfilled, not because it was inevitable, but because enough people acted as though it was. The prophecy wrote itself.

The stock market is another fertile ground for this paradox. Investors are not just reacting to fundamentals, they are reacting to what they believe other investors believe. If a large enough group believes a stock will fall, they may sell early. This collective action causes the very dip they feared. The decline, once only a possibility, becomes a reality because it was anticipated. The prophecy, fueled by nothing but speculation, manifests. Traders call it a "self-fulfilling prophecy," but in truth, it is the economy behaving like a mirror. It reflects belief as reality.

This paradox shows up in relationships, careers, and self-image. A person told as a child that they will never amount to anything may spend years doubting their value. Even with talent and opportunity, their inner narrative shapes their decisions. They hesitate. They play small. They sabotage good things. Over time, failure appears to confirm the original belief. It seems like the prophecy was true all along. But it was not. It was built piece by piece, day by day, by the very fear of its truth.

This is the cruel genius of the paradox. The more energy someone gives to trying to disprove a negative prediction, the more likely they are to act in ways that resemble it. Confidence gets replaced by defensiveness. Clarity turns to anxiety. When every step is taken with fear of what might happen, it becomes difficult to choose boldly. And without boldness, outcomes often spiral into exactly what was feared. Not because the world conspired against the person, but because fear narrowed their range of motion.

Entire populations can become caught in this cycle. A public warned endlessly that a leader will become a dictator may become hypervigilant, interpreting every action as evidence of tyranny. Protests erupt. Cracks appear in public order. The leader, now under siege, tightens control. What may have been a moderate administration now becomes paranoid, defensive, and aggressive, shaped by the very reactions of those who feared it. Again, belief drives behavior, and behavior alters reality.

It is tempting to dismiss these outcomes as coincidence, but the deeper truth is harder to ignore. Human systems, financial, social, political, are sensitive to perception. They are not machines. They are networks of people, reacting not only to facts but to feelings about what those facts might mean. When a forecast becomes widely known, it alters the environment. The forecast does not exist in a vacuum. It changes the landscape it claims to describe.

The paradox deepens when the prophecy appears benevolent. A person told they are destined for greatness may become driven, ambitious, and relentless. They study longer, work harder, and recover faster from failure. Their belief in a great future gives them energy that others lack. And in time, they may become exactly what they believed. But was that greatness truly written into their DNA, or was it built by their belief in a narrative that pushed them to rise?

This paradox is neither positive nor negative. It is simply a function of how belief interacts with behavior. Prophecies are not limited to ancient stories or supernatural claims. They are everywhere, in economic forecasts, in doctor's predictions, in standardized tests, in family expectations. What someone believes about themselves or their future changes how they act, and how they act changes what becomes true. Fate, in this sense, is not a script but a mirror.

Even silence can trigger the prophecy loop. If someone is told early on that they will be alone forever, they may become guarded. They avoid vulnerability, they mistrust compliments, they fear attachment. These habits, formed to protect against heartbreak, ironically ensure it. The loneliness was never a certainty, it was a possibility that became real because it was believed. The prophecy shaped the very behaviors that brought it to life.

This does not mean that every outcome is within human control. There are forces beyond belief, war, disease, disaster, injustice, that alter lives regardless of how anyone feels. But within the margin of what can be influenced, belief often plays a quiet but decisive role. People are not always living out their destiny. Sometimes they are just living out what they were told to expect.

The most powerful prophecies are not shouted. They are whispered repeatedly until they become part of the background. A student who hears that their school has low standards may stop trying. A worker who is told that no one ever gets promoted may stop asking. These are not declarations of truth. They are statements of expectation. And when adopted, they silently guide decisions, until they resemble truth.

To escape this paradox, learning to question the prophecy, not just the source but the behavior it shapes. Is this outcome truly inevitable, or am I preparing for it in ways that make it more likely? Is my caution really neutral, or is it feeding the thing I fear? These are difficult questions, but necessary ones. Without them, people sleepwalk through self-fulfilling traps, convinced that fate had the final say.

The paradox of the prophecy that writes itself is not about mysticism. It is about feedback loops. It is about how the mind influences the hand, and how the hand shapes the world. Belief, once embedded in behavior, becomes part of the system. The prophecy is no longer a prediction. It is a blueprint. And unless questioned, it is followed without resistance.

This is the strange truth: fate often begins as fiction. But fiction, when believed deeply enough, can become the foundation of fact. That is the power of a prophecy, not that it knows what will happen, but that it makes people behave as if it does.

A society convinced that automation will destroy all jobs may begin to withdraw investment from training programs, public education, and job creation. The narrative of inevitable collapse leads to real collapse. The prophecy becomes not just a reaction to external forces, but a roadmap people follow into their own undoing. Not because machines took over, but because people stopped preparing for anything else.

This is what makes the prophecy paradox so difficult to challenge. It is not an external force. It is internal. It is reinforced not through coercion but through subtle shifts in thought, behavior, and expectation. People act cautiously when they believe disaster is coming. They withhold trust. They lower their ambitions. They shrink their presence in the world. In trying to avoid failure, they inadvertently help create the conditions that guarantee it.

Many people carry unspoken prophecies given to them in childhood. These are not written on scrolls or delivered by divine figures. They are absorbed through comments, comparisons, and silence. A child who grows up hearing that they are a burden learns to anticipate rejection. They may walk into rooms assuming they are unwelcome. They might avoid asking for help, afraid it proves the point. Over time, they isolate themselves, not because no one cared, but because the prophecy made them act like it.

This makes personal development deeply challenging. You are not only working against your circumstances. You are also working against the mental scripts you were handed, sometimes decades ago, that quietly tell you what to expect. Even if life changes externally, these internal expectations can stay the same. Someone who becomes successful may still sabotage their happiness because they never believed it was sustainable. In their mind, the prophecy of failure still waits, still whispers, and still feels truer than the life they now live.

There are real costs to this. Potential is lost. People step back from opportunities they could have handled. They stay in relationships they have outgrown because they believe they cannot do better. They accept unfair treatment because they were told not to expect more. These choices do not come from weakness. They come from the invisible pull of prophecy, a force that shapes not what is real, but what is believed to be real.

Prophecy does not have to be spoken to hold power. It can be inherited through culture, reinforced by media, or passed down through patterns of behavior. Entire communities can adopt prophecies of decline, victimhood, or limitation. When generation after generation sees itself through a lens of restriction, it becomes harder to imagine anything else. Dreams are filtered through the prophecy before they ever reach reality. Possibilities shrink. Hope feels naïve. And change becomes something that happens to others, not to them.

The irony is that most people do not recognize they are following a prophecy at all. They believe they are just being realistic. They point to past examples as proof. They treat prior patterns as unbreakable laws. But this is another piece of the paradox: past results are often used as evidence that the future is fixed, even though it is human behavior that continues to repeat those outcomes. The prophecy appears true not because it was inevitable, but because it was modeled, copied, and passed forward.

This cycle is rarely broken by accident. It usually requires confrontation. Someone has to pause and ask: where did this idea come from? Who told me this was my fate? Is it mine to accept, or just the one I was handed? These questions are uncomfortable because they force people to look directly at the gap between what they believe and what they have chosen. The moment you identify a prophecy as just a suggestion, you weaken its hold.

The workplace is another domain where this paradox plays out. Employees who are labeled early on as "not management material" may internalize the message. They stop volunteering for leadership roles. They defer to others, even when they have better ideas. Over time, they are passed over for promotions, not because they lacked the skill, but because they stopped positioning themselves as ready. The label became a lens. The lens shaped behavior. The behavior confirmed the label.

It works in the opposite direction too. Someone labeled a rising star might get more attention, more mentoring, and more opportunities. Their confidence grows. They take on risk. Their upward trajectory becomes a kind of prophecy fulfilled. But again, was it destiny, or simply an amplified response to early belief? The difference matters because it means success is not only about ability, it is about perception, timing, and belief systems that act long before skill is fully measured.

This is why predictions must be handled with care. Every forecast is also a suggestion. And suggestions, when repeated and reinforced, begin to feel like truth. Whether you are a parent, a teacher, a manager, or a friend, the words you use to describe someone's future can plant seeds that shape more than feelings. They shape decisions. They shape effort. They shape resilience. Over time, they shape outcomes. This is not just about optimism. It is about responsibility.

Even scientific predictions are not immune to this paradox. A medical diagnosis, especially one tied to life expectancy, can trigger emotional responses that affect a patient's outcome. Someone told they have six months to live may begin to shut down socially, emotionally, even physically. But that estimate was never a guarantee. It was a probability based on past data. Still, if believed too deeply, it can function like a prophecy. And the patient, no longer fighting, may accelerate their own decline. The body follows the mind.

That is not to say that people should ignore forecasts, or pretend everything is under their control. But there is a difference between preparation and surrender. There is a line between using information to plan wisely and allowing it to become a script that replaces agency. That line is often crossed when belief overrides flexibility, when people assume that deviation is impossible, and when imagination gives way to resignation.

Young people from marginalized backgrounds are often treated as future threats rather than current individuals. They are punished more harshly, monitored more closely, and given fewer chances to recover from mistakes. These actions, based on a belief about what they are likely to become, often push them into the very outcomes that society feared. What began as a prediction becomes a sentence. The prophecy is fulfilled by the system that claimed to prevent it.

This is why changing the outcome of a prophecy requires more than hope. It requires an active refusal to let belief dictate behavior.

It demands that people hold room for what could be, not just what has been. It requires leaders to recognize how their assumptions shape policy, how parents shape identity, how narratives shape reality. Otherwise, we continue living in worlds built not by truth, but by expectation.

The Choice That Was Never Yours

Choice is one of the most deeply held values in modern society. People are told they can be anything, do anything, go anywhere, as long as they make the right decisions. The narrative of freedom is built into everything from politics to marketing. Buy this, vote for that, pursue this path, turn away from that one, because you are in control. You are the one who chooses. But beneath the surface, many of those so-called choices are already narrowed, shaped, or subtly coerced long before they reach the point of decision.

You believe you are steering the ship, but the map was drawn before you touched the wheel. The influences on your choices began years earlier, sometimes before you were even aware of the concept of decision-making. Culture, upbringing, trauma, reward systems, peer groups, economic class, gender roles, these do not just influence what you choose. They influence what you even perceive as available to choose.

It is easy to point to a moment and say, "That was my decision." But the scaffolding of that decision is rarely examined. Did you really choose your career, or did you follow what was praised in your household? Did you fall in love, or were you pulled toward what matched your template of familiarity? Did you walk away from a situation because it was wrong, or because you were taught that enduring discomfort is weakness? The mechanics of choice are rarely neutral.

People often underestimate how much of their "freedom" is actually preloaded. A person raised in scarcity may choose security over risk again and again, not because it is objectively better, but because their nervous system has been trained to avoid uncertainty. Another person raised with financial comfort may choose to start a business or travel abroad, believing they are brave or adventurous. But much of that courage was purchased by insulation from consequences. The decision feels free, but the conditions that made it possible were not universal.

This becomes more obvious in environments where real freedom is stripped away. A worker is told they can leave if they do not like their job, but they cannot afford rent without it. A student is told they can drop a class if they are overwhelmed, but doing so would delay their graduation and increase their debt. A citizen is told they are free to protest, but the law restricts where, when, and how, and the penalties are steep. These are not choices. They are obligations disguised as options.

Even outside of oppressive systems, the range of choice is often narrower than it appears. Algorithms now shape what people see, which influences what they think about, which determines what they choose. When every feed is personalized, every ad targeted, and every piece of information filtered, the sense of freedom becomes increasingly artificial. You may feel like you are exploring freely, but you are walking inside a walled garden, one designed to steer you toward predictable behavior.

Marketing preys on this illusion with precision. You are not just shown a product. You are shown a version of yourself who already owns it. The language is not commanding, it is suggestive. It whispers, "People like you already want this." The suggestion feels internal, as if you arrived at it yourself. But the truth is that you were guided. Your preferences were studied, your patterns mapped, and your behavior anticipated. What looks like a decision was often a funnel.

This is not always sinister. Suggestion is part of learning, culture, and communication. But the problem begins when people lose the ability to distinguish between what they want and what they were taught to want. That blur becomes especially dangerous when it feeds systems of inequality. If a person raised in a high-crime neighborhood chooses not to trust law enforcement, is that truly a free choice? Or is it the only logical response to lived experience? If a child grows up surrounded by failure, low expectations, and instability, do they really "choose" to underachieve, or is that outcome embedded in the ecosystem around them?

The modern obsession with personal responsibility often skips this step. People are told to own their choices, regardless of what shaped them. If someone fails, it is assumed they lacked discipline or vision. If someone succeeds, they are treated as inherently exceptional. But these conclusions ignore the invisible architecture of influence. They pretend that everyone stands at the same fork in the road. In reality, some people never even see certain paths. Some doors were locked before they arrived. Some were never built at all.

This is not an excuse to abandon accountability. Choices do matter. But the conversation about choice must be honest. It must account for structural bias, early conditioning, and psychological priming. Otherwise, society rewards the illusion of merit while punishing those who were never given access to the same stage. It becomes a game of blaming individuals for outcomes that were shaped by environments far beyond their control.

In relationships, this illusion plays out in painful ways. Someone may feel they chose a partner freely, but the qualities that drew them in were shaped by unresolved dynamics from their past.

A pattern of choosing emotionally distant people may not be a preference, but a reenactment of an unmet need. When that person gets hurt, they may blame themselves for "choosing wrong." But they were not choosing with full clarity. They were choosing through the lens of their wounds.

Therapists often refer to these patterns as unconscious scripts. They are behavioral loops that repeat until they are made conscious. A person may switch cities, jobs, or relationships repeatedly, believing each time that this is a fresh start. But unless the underlying script is examined, the same outcome plays out. Different names, different faces, same story. The person may feel cursed or unlucky. In truth, they are reenacting a script that was never questioned. The choices feel new. But the driver behind them is ancient.

This raises uncomfortable questions about free will. If so much of human behavior is reactive, shaped by the past, driven by emotion, manipulated by algorithms, and limited by circumstance, then what part of choice is truly independent? The answer may lie not in the decision itself, but in the level of awareness brought to it. The more conscious someone becomes of their influences, the more deliberate their choices can be. Awareness does not eliminate all pressure, but it creates space between impulse and action.

This space is where true choice lives. Not in the absence of influence, but in the recognition of it. A person who knows they were taught to fear failure can pause and ask whether that fear is still serving them. A person who recognizes that their attraction to chaos comes from childhood instability can learn to choose peace, even if it feels unfamiliar. These choices are not automatic. They require effort, reflection, and often discomfort. But they are more real than the ones made by default.

The more people are taught to think critically, the better they become at identifying manipulation, bias, and inherited belief. A population that understands how systems shape decisions is harder to control. That is why oppressive regimes often suppress education or control the narrative. They fear what happens when people begin to ask, "Did I really choose this?"

Even in freedom-loving societies, this question is uncomfortable. If large swaths of people begin to recognize that their consumption habits, political affiliations, and personal identities were shaped by unseen forces, the foundations of that society begin to tremble. What happens when a citizen realizes they were never really voting for change, just for a different face on the same system? What happens when a worker sees that their career path was not a ladder of success, but a treadmill of compliance? These realizations are not easy to digest. But they are necessary.

The goal is not to eliminate influence. That is impossible. The goal is to expose it. To make it visible. Once a person sees the levers being pulled, they can begin to resist. They can pause before buying, speaking, voting, or reacting. They can ask, "Where is this coming from?" That moment of pause is the seed of real autonomy. It is the beginning of ownership, not just of the decision, but of the forces that shaped it.

When people begin to question the choices they once made without hesitation, it can feel destabilizing. Regret often emerges. "Why did I waste years doing this?" "How could I not have seen it?" But this regret is not weakness. It is the sign of awakening. It is what happens when a person moves from passive participant to active agent. The key is not to drown in guilt, but to use that awareness as a foundation for a new kind of decision-making, one informed by understanding, not assumption.

This is not a call to abandon structure or tradition. Some inherited ideas are valuable. Some systems work. But even valuable traditions must be chosen, not simply followed. A belief repeated without reflection is not wisdom. It is habit. And habit, when it masquerades as choice, becomes a cage.

Fighting Fate, Fulfilling It

There is something heroic about resistance. The idea that a person can rise up and defy what others expect of them is embedded in nearly every story that inspires. The underdog, the rebel, the outcast, these figures are glorified not for their compliance, but for their defiance. They are remembered for saying no when others said yes, for breaking free when the path ahead was clear and limiting. But within many of these stories is a contradiction that is easy to overlook: in trying to escape their supposed destiny, they often run directly into it. The very act of fighting fate becomes the force that fulfills it.

This is not just literary drama. It plays out in real life with haunting regularity. People sometimes devote their entire lives to avoiding one outcome, only to arrive at it through the back door. A person who is desperate not to become their parents may spend so much energy pushing in the opposite direction that they fail to notice when they adopt the same patterns under different names. The fear of repeating history becomes the compass, and eventually, the destination. Not because the outcome was inescapable, but because the fight against it was so consuming that it replaced thoughtful direction.

This is the paradox: intense resistance can produce alignment. When your identity is built around not becoming something, you are still shaped by that thing. You orbit it. You measure against it. You make decisions through its lens. Even if you take a different path, your focus on it ensures that it remains central. The map may change, but the coordinates of origin remain fixed.

Movements built entirely on opposition often suffer the same fate. A group rises to destroy what came before, determined not to replicate the errors of the past. But without a clear, stable vision of what they stand for, their rebellion becomes reactive rather than constructive. They define themselves by what they reject, not what they create. Over time, they become disorganized, bitter, and eventually authoritarian, the very structure they claimed to oppose. The energy spent fighting the old system becomes the seed of the new one, just as rigid, just as broken.

This pattern often appears in relationships. Someone who witnessed emotional neglect in their early years may vow never to experience it again. They may become fiercely independent, avoidant, and hyper-aware of red flags. But in doing so, they also push away intimacy. They avoid vulnerability, interpret kindness as manipulation, and leave before being left. In trying to protect themselves from the fate of being hurt, they ensure it. Their self-imposed isolation becomes indistinguishable from the very loneliness they sought to avoid.

This kind of resistance is not always conscious. Many people believe they are exercising control, reclaiming power, or making smart choices. And in some ways, they are. But when every decision is rooted in opposition rather than direction, the person becomes reactive, not sovereign. They are not navigating. They are avoiding it. And avoidance is not a strategy. It is a form of surrender disguised as effort.

Some of the most painful human experiences come from watching someone struggle against a fate they do not realize they are fulfilling. A person swears they will never be poor, and works themselves into exhaustion chasing financial security, only to destroy their health and relationships in the process. Another declares they will never be weak, and spends years hardening themselves emotionally, becoming closed, aggressive, and brittle. Both believed they were escaping failure. Both ended up replicating it through different means.

This paradox is not a punishment. It is a result of misdirected energy. When someone commits to "never becoming" something, they often fail to define what they do want. Their life becomes a series of reactions. They are constantly looking over their shoulder, preparing for the ghost of what they fear. But the brain cannot live in reverse. It needs forward motion. Without it, people become trapped in patterns that feel purposeful, but are actually defensive.

True freedom does not come from rebellion. It comes from clarity. The person who breaks free of a harmful pattern does not just resist it, they replace it. They study what went wrong, name what they need, and choose deliberately rather than impulsively. Their life becomes guided by vision, not vengeance. Without that shift, the fight continues indefinitely, and the original fate remains close.

In generational cycles, this paradox becomes even more powerful. A parent who grew up in neglect may become overprotective, determined to give their children everything they never had. But in overcorrecting, they may prevent their children from developing resilience. The child grows up unprepared for hardship, lacking basic problem-solving skills, and struggles when life inevitably becomes difficult. The parent tried to prevent suffering. Instead, they postponed and reshaped it. Their child faces different problems, but ones rooted in the same origin: imbalance.

This cycle is difficult to break because it often feels like progress. When your life looks different than the one you escaped, you assume you have changed the outcome. But transformation is not about surface changes. It is about internal shifts. A new job, a new city, or a new relationship does not matter if your thinking, fears, and patterns remain the same. You may fight your past with everything you have, only to discover you carried it with you into the future.

The key to breaking this loop is to stop treating fate as a fixed opponent. Not everything you fear is waiting to trap you. Not every failure is inevitable. But when you move through life with that assumption, you set up a combative posture that narrows your range of options. You become suspicious of possibility. You look for hidden traps at every opportunity. And in doing so, you miss the very exits that could have freed you.

Cultural narratives often reinforce this problem. Stories glorify the fighter, the escape artist, the one who burns the old world to the ground. But they rarely show what comes next. What happens after the system is destroyed? What happens after the person walks away? If the answer is nothing but silence, isolation, or collapse, then the rebellion was only half the battle. Without construction, resistance turns to ruin.

This is why healing is not just about opposition. It is about intention. It is not enough to say what you do not want. You must also know what you are moving toward. Otherwise, you spend your life dodging shadows and mistaking movement for progress. You become skilled at defending yourself from a threat that may no longer be present. And in the process, you miss the fact that your own defenses are now the threat.

This paradox is particularly dangerous in leadership. A person who rises to power after years of being ignored or underestimated may promise to lead differently. But if their leadership is fueled by resentment, they may replicate the very systems they hated. They surround themselves with loyalists, silence criticism, and punish dissent, all under the banner of change. What they resisted becomes what they now enforce. And because they see themselves as the antidote to the past, they struggle to admit when they have become its continuation.

The illusion that you are breaking a cycle simply because you are struggling against it is one of the most persistent traps in personal growth. Resistance can feel virtuous. It can feel righteous. But without reflection, it becomes a kind of blindness. You end up following the same road, just in reverse. You avoid one outcome so intensely that you run past the path you truly needed, and arrive at the very destination you feared.

Instead of asking what you are running from, ask what you are running toward. Instead of defining your identity in contrast to what hurt you, define it by your values, your priorities, your vision. Build a life that is not just a rejection of the past, but an invitation to something better.

Fate is not always a prison. But when your energy is consumed entirely by resisting it, you lose the ability to choose anything else. You fight, you exhaust yourself, and you collapse into the arms of the very thing you swore you would never become. Not because it won, but because you never learned to stop fighting long enough to walk away.

The Fork That Never Split

Step back far enough, and complexity begins to collapse. Systems that once appeared distinct start to resemble each other. Separate movements, divided ideologies, competing frameworks, they all begin to spiral into a shared center. From a distance, the road looks full of options. But step back far enough, and the terrain flattens into one continuous path.

What you thought were different roads were often variations in texture, not direction.

The human mind favors contrast. It needs to categorize, to label difference as evidence of progress. But much of what appears divergent is unified beneath the surface. Apparent separation is often a function of scale. The closer you are to the decision point, the more distinct the options seem. Only when you observe the entire pattern do you realize that the outcome was not defined by the branches, it was defined by the root.

Civilizations have fractured over doctrine, symbols, and storylines, convinced that their paths diverged. But behind the flags and banners, the structure often repeated. Authority grew, language codified control, systems centralized power, and belief hardened into law. It did not matter which banner was raised. The pattern beneath the banner remained. The illusion of separation served to energize the participants, but the result, again and again, was uniform: consolidation, hierarchy, collapse.

This is not cynicism. It is symmetry.

Throughout history, opposition has served as a mirror more than a wall. Every resistance gives shape to the thing it opposes. In trying to define itself, it reinforces the boundaries of its rival. Competing schools of thought borrow each other's vocabulary. Rigidly divided frameworks use the same scaffolding under different terms. What was once a fork becomes a spiral, each side chasing the other's definition until the lines blur.

Even identity behaves this way. What begins as divergence, a break from what came before, often resolves into mimicry. A new identity is formed, not in isolation, but in reaction. Its language is defined by the one it left. Its symbols are crafted in contrast to what it rejected. But the underlying structure is still shaped by that origin. The fork appears wide, but the angle of separation narrows with every step.

You do not need to go far to see this convergence. Even in systems designed to maximize difference, in art, philosophy, or technology, the underlying pressures remain consistent. Scarcity, attention, recognition, influence. Over time, the system corrects creative divergence into profitable sameness. Novelty is absorbed, branded, and folded back into the framework it once tried to disrupt. The branch returns to the trunk.

What this reveals is not that difference is false, but that difference alone does not guarantee redirection. The existence of multiple paths does not mean those paths lead to different destinations. Many systems are engineered to simulate branching while directing all movement toward a shared outcome, stability, conformity, containment.

The paradox is that the appearance of choice strengthens the system. It makes participation feel voluntary. When people see multiple routes, they are less likely to question whether the terrain itself has been designed. The fork keeps them engaged. The subtle convergence keeps them contained.

In this way, the fork that never split is not a trick, it is a mechanism. It is how complex systems maintain coherence without appearing rigid. It is how power structures offer difference without allowing deviation. It is how outcomes are shaped before action begins.

If you want to escape a pattern, you cannot rely on difference. You must study structure. You must ask whether the roads before you are truly divergent, or simply dressed to appear so. The only way to move toward a different outcome is to leave the frame entirely, not to walk a new path within it, but to question whether the frame should exist at all.

The fork was never the point.

The Truth That Changes Nothing

The Revelation That Left Everything Intact

A secret finally told. A fact uncovered after years of denial. A hidden motive brought to light. And yet, nothing changes.

The people who should have left do not leave. The systems that should have collapsed do not shake. The behaviors that should have stopped continue without interruption. The revelation arrives like a stone meant to shatter glass, but it lands without sound. Everything stays in place.

There is no resistance. There is no denial. The truth is accepted, acknowledged, even repeated. But it is not acted upon. It settles into the world as if it were always there. The impact is absorbed, not because it was small, but because the world around it refuses to rearrange. This is the paradox, that something can be real, provable, and even devastating, and still be irrelevant.

We expect that truth has weight. That once revealed, it will demand a response. That once spoken, it will force reorganization. But the revelation that leaves everything intact shows that truth is not powerful on its own. Its effect depends on the willingness of people and systems to respond. When that willingness is absent, truth becomes a decoration. Present, but meaningless.

You see it in the person who discovers their partner's betrayal and still comes home each night pretending they never found out. Not because they misunderstand what happened, but because they understand it too well. They know what the truth requires, the conversations, the decisions, the unraveling, and they decide against it. So the truth is buried under silence. Not denial, but a deliberate kind of paralysis. The knowledge is real, but the consequences are rejected.

It is easy to label that as a flaw. But often, it is calculation. People weigh what truth will cost and choose comfort over confrontation. The lie is easier than the fallout of clarity. So they let the truth sit beside them and live around it. It becomes part of the background noise. That is how revelations fade without ever exploding.

In larger structures, this paradox grows sharper. Consider what happens when internal corruption is exposed within a powerful institution. The data is undeniable. The actions were unethical, even illegal. Investigations are launched. Apologies are crafted. A few policies are rewritten. But the institution remains. The same people sit in charge. The same behaviors repeat under different names.

This is not a failure to understand the problem. It is refusal to dismantle the structure that caused it. The revelation arrived, but no one was truly waiting for it. It was received like a guest who stays too long, tolerated, but not welcomed.

The effect is worse than ignorance. Because now everyone knows, and nothing is different.

The idea that truth brings justice, or healing, or redemption, is more comfortable than real. In practice, truth is often inconvenient. It disrupts order. It demands change. And when people are not ready for that change ,or benefit from avoiding it, they absorb the truth and then ignore it.

This explains why confessions do not always lead to forgiveness. Why exposure does not always lead to downfall. Why revolutions begin with truth, but rarely survive on it. The world is full of people who understand exactly what is wrong, and still do nothing.

The revelation happened. The silence that followed was louder.

The Burden of Knowing

There are truths that set people free. And there are truths that trap them in place.

Not because they are unclear, but because they are too clear. Some people carry knowledge that isolates them. Not just facts or information, but an understanding of how things work, how people behave, and what patterns never change. That kind of awareness does not always bring peace. For many, it creates pressure. It separates them from others. It turns intelligence into a source of exhaustion.

The burden of knowing begins when you realize that the more you understand, the harder it is to speak simply, to live normally, or to relate comfortably. Conversations feel shallow. Reassurances feel dishonest. And the systems around you start to look rigged in ways others either cannot see or refuse to acknowledge.

Knowing too much can make it harder to participate in everyday life, not because you are smarter than others, but because you are no longer able to believe the same things they do.

That is the foundation of this paradox. We are taught to believe that awareness is always a gift. But past a certain point, it becomes something else. It becomes isolating. It becomes heavy. The person who sees too clearly begins to detach, not out of pride, but because the gap between what they know and what others accept grows too wide to cross.

Some people become quiet. Others become bitter. A few go insane.

And most of them never get recognized for what they are truly struggling with, not failure, not confusion, but the silent cost of understanding too much in a world that prefers distraction.

People tend to assume that the hardest part of intelligence is the pressure to perform. That gifted students burn out from expectations, or that highly capable adults feel weighed down by responsibility. But that is only one part of the truth. The deeper burden comes from disconnection, from being unable to turn your mind off, from constantly analyzing things others overlook, from always seeing five steps ahead in situations where others are only reacting to the present.

At first, this can feel like a strength. But over time, it begins to separate you from your surroundings. When your awareness reaches a level where you can no longer accept convenient answers or participate in common illusions, a quiet detachment starts to form. You smile less. You engage less. Not because you want to isolate yourself, but because the effort to stay connected to something that no longer feels real begins to wear you down.

In many cases, this disconnection begins early. Children who are unusually perceptive often notice tension adults try to hide. They see hypocrisy in rules meant to simplify behavior. They ask questions that make others uncomfortable, not to challenge authority, but because the logic they are given does not line up with what they observe. These children are not trying to rebel. They are trying to understand.

But when understanding is not welcomed, it starts to become internal. They learn to stop asking questions out loud. They begin keeping their thoughts to themselves. They observe quietly, process deeply, and drift into their own world. From the outside, they appear withdrawn. But inside, they are simply carrying too much awareness and too little connection.

As they grow older, this gap widens. They begin to realize that most people do not want to be understood, they want to be agreed with. That most conversations are rituals, not exchanges. That most institutions are built to protect appearances, not to solve real problems. Once they know this, it becomes difficult to un-know it. Participation becomes performance. And performance becomes exhausting.

This is how intelligence becomes suffering.

There is also a physical toll to this kind of knowledge. The nervous system adapts to constant awareness by staying alert. A person who notices every detail, questions every motive, and predicts every outcome cannot easily relax. Their mind does not rest. It loops, revisits, rechecks. They struggle with sleep. They anticipate problems before they arise. They carry invisible tension in their body that never fully dissolves.

And when they try to explain this, they are often misunderstood. Others may think they are anxious, overreacting, or pessimistic. But the person is not imagining things. They are seeing real patterns, real signals, real risks. The issue is not that they are wrong, it is that they are early. And being early in awareness often feels like being alone in a crowd that refuses to look up.

Eventually, some people give up on trying to explain. They stop bringing things up. They stop trying to warn others. They stop hoping to be understood. Their intelligence becomes internalized, folded into private routines and silent observations. On the outside, they may seem calm. But it is the calm of someone who no longer expects the world to meet them where they are.

History is full of examples of brilliant minds who collapsed under the weight of their own awareness. Some were artists, some were scientists, some were philosophers. What they shared was not just intelligence, but sensitivity, a depth of perception that made the world harder to bear. Their suffering was not rooted in confusion, but in clarity. They understood things too well. And because of that, they struggled to live inside a reality that refused to reflect what they saw.

Friedrich Nietzsche was one of them. A philosopher whose insights into morality, power, and human behavior were decades ahead of his time, but who ultimately fell into madness. His writings were sharp, his ideas radical, and his mind unrelenting. He dissected every system he encountered, including himself. But in the end, the weight of his understanding detached him from reality altogether. He did not die from disease alone. He died from a mind that could no longer carry what it saw.

There are modern versions of this too. People who begin with brilliance and end with breakdown. Not because they lacked coping skills, but because they lived in a constant state of cognitive overload. When your mind cannot stop processing, when your insights isolate you from connection, and when the world punishes you for being right too early, collapse is not a failure, it is a consequence.

Even outside the extremes, this burden shows up in more subtle ways. You see it in people who are always five seconds ahead in conversation, but struggle to enjoy it. In those who solve problems at work before anyone else recognizes them, but are resented for speaking up. In those who understand the motives behind a compliment or an insult and cannot take either at face value. They are not trying to be difficult. They are simply unable to turn off the awareness that others never had to turn on.

Sometimes, these people try to downplay themselves. They learn to keep their thoughts shorter, their speech simpler, their questions less probing. They hide their depth because they have learned that truth, when spoken too clearly, can make others uncomfortable. They dull themselves not out of shame, but out of survival. It is easier to be accepted as average than to be exiled for being correct.

But pretending takes energy. And eventually, that energy runs out.

There is also emotional pain embedded in the burden of knowing. When you see people make the same mistakes over and over, and you understand exactly why they are doing it, but know they are not ready to hear the answer. When you recognize the long-term consequences of short-term decisions, but also know that no one will listen until it is too late. When you predict the outcome of a situation days or weeks ahead of time, and when it finally happens, you are not vindicated, you are just tired.

This kind of pain is not loud. It is quiet. It shows up in emotional detachment, in disinterest, in the flat tone of someone who no longer expects anyone to change. It shows up in sarcasm, in subtle resentment, in long silences during conversations where nothing honest can be said. It is not about feeling superior. It is about feeling stuck, trapped between understanding and action, insight and futility.

Because what do you do when you know the truth, but know that no one else wants it?

You either carry it alone, or you bury it with the rest of the things no one asked you to notice.

There is a phrase often repeated in education and psychology: "twice exceptional." It refers to individuals who are both gifted and challenged — brilliant in some ways, struggling in others. But the deeper truth is that those two conditions are not separate. Sometimes the struggle is born from the gift. High intelligence, high sensitivity, and high awareness come with costs that few people see from the outside.

These are not people with an advantage. They are people with a different weight to carry.

And the hardest part of carrying that weight is that it cannot be shared. It is not a visible injury. It is not a recognized diagnosis. It is a silent overload of constant thought, constant insight, and constant disconnection from the surface-level simplicity that most people are allowed to enjoy.

Some try to escape it. They distract themselves, dull their minds with routines, cling to entertainment or consumption to slow their thoughts. Others try to spiritualize their understanding, to make peace with it by seeing themselves as observers rather than participants. But most of them carry the same feeling — that knowing more has not made them feel more powerful. It has made them feel more alone.

The paradox is that understanding is supposed to bring control, but often brings disillusionment. It is supposed to offer protection, but often delivers isolation. It is supposed to make life richer, but sometimes makes it harder to live at all.

The burden of knowing is not just about what you see. It is about what you can no longer pretend not to see.

The Clarity That Closed the Door

There is a specific kind of stagnation that does not come from confusion, but from conviction.

Some people stop growing not because they are lost, but because they are certain. They reach a conclusion about the world, about another person, about a belief, and that conclusion becomes fixed. It is no longer open to questioning. No longer flexible. No longer vulnerable to evidence, conversation, or reflection. They have decided what is true, and that decision becomes the wall between who they are and who they could still become.

This is the paradox, that clarity, which is supposed to sharpen understanding, can sometimes harden it instead. When someone becomes too convinced that they are right, the possibility of becoming more right disappears. The search ends. The openness collapses. The mind, once fluid, locks. And the person may not even realize that what they call strength is actually stuckness.

The most common place this shows up is in arguments. Two people disagree. One raises their voice. The other sharpens their tone. Each becomes more certain as the conversation continues, not because the other side is wrong, but because the act of defending themselves requires that they become right. Pride tightens. Ego inflates. And before the discussion even finishes, the outcome is sealed. They will leave the conversation more rigid than they entered it.

What began as a disagreement ends as a dead end.

Not because one of them won, but because both of them closed the door.

It is easy to assume that clarity always helps resolve things. But in practice, what most people call clarity is often a performance of certainty. It is not clarity based on new insight. It is clarity built on the need to win, the fear of being challenged, or the emotional comfort of sticking to a conclusion that protects identity.

There is a cost to always being sure. When someone builds their self-image around being right, about politics, religion, relationships, morality, they stop learning. Every disagreement becomes a threat. Every challenge becomes personal. And every new piece of information is filtered through the question, "Does this confirm what I already believe?"

If it does not, it is dismissed. Not because it lacks merit, but because it risks opening the door they already closed.

This kind of thinking does not look like ignorance. It often looks like intelligence. These people can be articulate, well-read, and persuasive. But underneath the surface is a mind that is no longer porous. It has become a sealed room, decorated with facts, but untouched by change.

The door is shut. And not because there is nothing more to learn, but because the person no longer wants to learn it.

This door often closes at the exact moment when growth is possible. The person encounters an idea that challenges them. A relationship that reveals their blind spots. A situation that contradicts their assumptions. The opportunity for evolution is right there. But instead of stepping forward, they shut down. They double down. They reinforce their position not because it is the strongest, but because it is the most familiar.

They mistake stability for strength. They mistake rigidity for integrity.

And once that mistake is made, the rest of life bends around it. Relationships are filtered through it. Information is reshaped to fit it. And any discomfort that threatens it is labeled as ignorance, immorality, or irrelevance.

Ego plays a central role here. To change your mind, you must first admit that your previous view was incomplete. That admission threatens pride. It creates vulnerability. And in a culture that rewards quick takes, strong opinions, and constant confidence, vulnerability looks like weakness. So people learn not to show it. They learn to perform certainty, even when they quietly doubt. Over time, the performance becomes a habit. And the habit becomes identity.

The tragedy is not that people are wrong. It is that they stop being open to the idea that they could be.

In this way, certainty becomes a kind of self-imposed exile. It feels like power, but it disconnects you from growth, complexity, and collaboration. You build a house made of your conclusions, and then find yourself stuck inside it, unable to hear, unable to shift, unable to leave.

You see this play out in movements and ideologies all the time. What begins as a search for truth becomes a declaration of it. What begins as curiosity turns into dogma. The members of a cause become so sure they are morally correct that they no longer examine their methods, their assumptions, or their impact. Any internal questioning is seen as betrayal. Any external criticism is labeled as ignorance or evil.

The original idea may have been noble. But the refusal to question it turns it into something brittle, something dangerous. Because once a group becomes convinced they are absolutely right, they become capable of justifying anything in the name of protecting that certainty.

That is how truth becomes violence. How justice becomes punishment. How conviction becomes cruelty.

All because a door was closed, not by truth, but by pride disguised as truth.

The consequences are quiet but devastating. A person gets hurt in a relationship and decides they now understand how people are. They form conclusions about trust, love, and commitment. These beliefs harden. The next time someone tries to get close to them, they are already measuring that person against the assumptions they decided years ago were facts.

They are no longer seeing the individual. They are seeing a confirmation or violation of their previous clarity.

The door is closed. And no matter how kind or genuine the new person may be, they are already shut out by history the moment they knock.

That is how people stay lonely without knowing it. That is how people keep repeating the same stories, with different names. The problem is not the world. The problem is that the door that might let the world in was locked a long time ago, and the key was the belief, "I already know."

One of the most dangerous sentences a person can carry is:

"That's just how it is."

Not because it is always wrong, but because it often signals the end of thinking. The end of trying. The end of possibility. It is a phrase used not to describe reality, but to protect someone from having to rethink it. It sounds wise. But it often hides defeat.

There is nothing weak about uncertainty. There is nothing shameful about adjusting your view. The strongest people are not those who defend the same position forever. They are the ones who update it when they discover it no longer fits.

Even when it means admitting you were wrong. Even when it means giving someone else the space to be right. That is where growth happens. That is where progress lives. And that is the paradox.

Sometimes, the clearest moment in your life is the one that stops you from ever seeing anything new again.

The Unmoving Truth

Some truths are hidden. Others are denied. But the most dangerous ones are the truths that everyone already knows, and no one moves to change.

These truths do not exist in the shadows. They are out in the open. They are discussed on news broadcasts, debated in classrooms, whispered in hallways, and embedded in policy reports. People nod when they are mentioned. They quote them. They reference them in speeches and articles and everyday conversation. And yet, despite all the awareness, despite the evidence and repetition, these truths do not shift. They remain in place. Still. Permanent. Unmoving.

This is the paradox: that the most visible truths are often the least touched. Not because they are misunderstood, but because they have already been accepted, and quietly given up on.

The most obvious example is inequality. It is not a secret that wealth is concentrated in the hands of a few. It is not controversial to point out that opportunity is distributed unevenly across lines of class, race, geography, and power. In fact, these facts are so well known that they have become clichés. People say things like "the rich get richer" or "the system is rigged" with a tone that suggests resignation, not outrage.

Everyone knows the truth. But the scale of the truth has made it untouchable.

The problem is not lack of awareness. It is saturation. The facts are repeated so often, so casually, that they lose their friction. They become background noise. People adjust their lives around them instead of through them. The imbalance is not confronted. It is normalized.

That is how injustice survives even after being exposed. It does not need to hide. It just needs to be old news.

This pattern plays out in institutions as well. A school system fails its students year after year. A healthcare system rewards profit over care. A justice system punishes the poor while protecting the powerful. These are not hidden failures. They are well-documented, thoroughly analyzed, and frequently criticized.

And yet, they remain.

There are reforms. There are task forces. There are headlines. But the core remains untouched. The root of the issue is not policy confusion or lack of data. The root is inertia. The systems are too large, the interests too embedded, the effort required too great. So instead of meaningful change, society offers symbolic movement, shifting surface details while leaving the foundation exactly where it was.

The truth is known. And because it is known, it becomes a kind of permission to stop trying.

In smaller ways, this shows up in personal life too. A person may recognize that their family dynamic is toxic. That their workplace is exploitative. That their relationship is fundamentally imbalanced. They do not deny it. They talk about it. They might even joke about it. The truth has already been integrated into their understanding of the situation.

But the truth does not move them. It becomes part of the structure of their life, acknowledged, but unchallenged.

This is not always a weakness. Sometimes it is the result of long, painful calculation. A person looks at what it would take to confront the truth, the fight, the loss, the uncertainty, and decides not to. They choose stability over honesty, endurance over transformation. The truth becomes something to live with, not something to live through.

And over time, that decision hardens into routine. The discomfort becomes familiar. The problem becomes permanent.

The person adapts to the truth instead of changing it.

There is something deeply human about this pattern. People are not built to constantly react to everything they know. If they did, life would become unbearable. And so the mind finds ways to coexist with contradiction. It learns how to hold uncomfortable facts without letting them interfere too much. It builds compartments. It creates distance. It teaches people how to speak truths they will never act on.

This is why it is possible for entire societies to acknowledge brutal facts without collapsing under the weight of them. The knowledge is there, but it has been neutralized.

The unmoving truth is not a mystery. It is a monument. It stands in the open, surrounded by people who believe in its importance, and who also accept its permanence.

Sometimes this phenomenon is labeled apathy. But that is too simple. What looks like apathy is often exhaustion. The truth has been fought before, and nothing changed. The protest happened. The article was written. The data was released. The calls were made. And the system did not move.

So the next time the truth comes up, it is met with a quieter response. Not denial, not anger, just a look that says, "Yes, we know."

That knowledge becomes a stopping point, not a starting point.

This is how movements die. Not through suppression, but through saturation. Not because people forget the truth, but because they cannot keep fighting for something that refuses to budge. The truth becomes a closed loop. It feeds itself. It survives, but it no longer provokes change.

It becomes something to agree with, not something to act on.

The media landscape reinforces this cycle. Outrage has a short shelf life. People consume information rapidly, then move on. Truths are presented like content, packaged, dramatized, and then replaced. A scandal lasts forty-eight hours. A tragedy is posted, shared, reacted to, and then drowned beneath the next one.

In this cycle, even the most important truths become temporary performances. They are amplified for a moment, then archived. The knowledge remains, but the urgency fades. The world moves, but the truth does not.

That is the cost of always being informed, the rare becomes routine. The extraordinary becomes expected. And the importance becomes inert.

There is a deeper danger here. When truth loses its ability to provoke change, people start turning to fiction that can. Conspiracies, myths, and simplified narratives become more attractive than the complicated reality that never seems to move. People would rather chase a lie that feels alive than sit with a truth that refuses to change.

That is how movements built on falsehood gain traction. Not because the truth was unavailable, but because it was available for too long, and never seemed to matter.

When truth becomes stagnant, belief becomes desperate.

It is tempting to blame institutions for this, but individuals do it too. People hold beliefs about themselves that are accurate and limiting. "I am not good with people." "I am always the problem." "I will never succeed." These statements are not dramatic. They are quiet, steady, deeply familiar.

And because the person has believed them for so long, they no longer question them. The truth, even if painful, becomes the framework of identity. It stops being a possibility to confront and becomes a rule to obey.

This internalized truth becomes unmoving not because it is true, but because it has never been truly tested.

And like all truths left unchallenged, it begins to feel like a fact of nature.

So what does it take to move an unmoving truth?

Sometimes it takes force. A shock to the system. A disruption too large to ignore. Other times it takes repetition, not of the truth itself, but of the actions that support it. Not just saying it again, but showing it differently.

But most of the time, the only thing that can move an unmoving truth is commitment. Not a flash of action, but the decision to persist even when nothing responds.

Because the paradox is this: the truth may not change the world immediately. But refusing to act on it guarantees that the world will never change at all.

Morality that divides

The Right Side That Refuses to Listen

In 1979, two Stanford psychologists ran an experiment that would go on to explain more about modern conflict than any political theory ever could. They gathered a group of students and presented them with a stack of mixed evidence about the death penalty. Some studies showed it worked as a deterrent. Others showed it had no effect at all. Every participant was exposed to the same data, same numbers, same language, same logic.

But the results did not push people toward agreement. The opposite happened.

Those who already believed in the death penalty became more convinced it worked. Those who opposed it became more convinced it did not. Confronted with the same facts, people became further divided. Not because the facts were unclear, but because they challenged the moral lens through which each person saw the world.

This is the paradox: the stronger a person believes they are right, especially morally right, the less likely they are to change their mind when shown evidence that contradicts them.

Not only do people resist opposing views, they often become more entrenched on their own when those views are presented. It is called belief polarization, and it explains why so many arguments about justice, fairness, or ethics lead nowhere. The very moment we feel we are on the "right side," we begin to lose the ability to hear anyone who might prove otherwise.

This is not an intellectual problem. It is a psychological one. When someone ties their moral identity to a belief, whether it is political, religious, or cultural, that belief becomes personal. Challenging it is no longer just an intellectual disagreement. It feels like an attack on character.

And when someone feels morally attacked, they rarely become more open. They become defensive. Their brain starts looking for ways to protect the identity that belief supports. Logic turns into armor. Conversation becomes a battlefield.

Even in private thought, the mind twists to keep moral certainty alive.

This is why intelligent, well-informed people can become the most stubborn. They are better at arguing. Better at collecting sources. Better at weaponizing facts. But the quality of the facts does not matter if the purpose is to defend rather than understand.

That is the difference between learning and positioning.

And it is why some of the fiercest conflicts today are not between people who are confused, but between people who believe they are doing good, and have stopped listening to anyone who disagrees.

What makes this paradox even more powerful is how often it plays out in spaces designed for dialogue. Classrooms, social platforms, even protests, places that claim to welcome open discussion often become stages for performance, not listening. Not because people are acting in bad faith, but because they come in with a fixed moral position that they believe should not be negotiated.

This creates a strange tension: people show up to engage, but only on terms that validate what they already believe. When those terms are not met, they withdraw or escalate. Listening becomes conditional. The conversation becomes conditional. You are only worth hearing if you are already close to agreement.

This is not how persuasion works. It is how division hardens.

At the center of this behavior is something deeper than ideology it is identity. People often do not defend ideas. They defend the version of themselves that those ideas support. If someone believes that their values make them a good person, then hearing an opposing view feels like more than disagreement. It feels like a suggestion that they are not who they think they are.

That is why even small moral disagreements can trigger disproportionate emotional reactions. A question about tone becomes a question about character. A disagreement about method becomes a claim about worth. The conversation is no longer about the issue. It is about the person.

And when the person feels attacked, their ability to hear collapses.

The Good That Turns Against Itself

Most harm does not begin with the desire to harm. It begins with the desire to help, to protect, to fix. People do not wake up eager to become the villain in someone else's story. More often, they begin with a sense of purpose, a desire to make something better, more just, more fair. But somewhere along the way, the mission overtakes morality. The intention stays good. The behavior no longer does.

This is the paradox: people trying to do the right thing can end up doing real damage, not because they abandoned their values, but because they held onto them too tightly.

You can see it in activism, where the urgency to create justice becomes a justification for cruelty. Where calling out wrong behavior slowly shifts into shaming people publicly for small mistakes. Where the cause becomes so sacred that there is no room for conversation, only correction. The goal was inclusion, but the method became exclusion. The goal was fairness, but the tone becomes punishment.

The energy that once aimed to heal ends up creating fear, the fear of saying the wrong thing, of asking the wrong question, of being misunderstood and cast out. People become more careful, but not more thoughtful. They are not growing. They are censoring themselves for survival.

The paradox is that the movement becomes morally intimidating, even to the people it was meant to protect.

This same pattern appears in religion. At its best, faith can ground a person in humility, compassion, and service. But when those values harden into rules, and those rules become more important than people, faith turns rigid. The moral core becomes legalistic.

And the harder someone tries to do "what is right," the more dangerous it becomes when they start believing they already know what that is in every situation, for every person.

Good intentions stop being flexible. They stop being curious. They turn into enforcement.

You also see this paradox clearly in parenting. Many parents deeply love their children and genuinely want what is best for them. But love alone does not prevent harm. Sometimes, it becomes the very excuse for it. A parent wants to protect their child from failure, so they begin controlling every decision. They want to make sure their child is kind, so they punish every emotion that does not look gentle. They want to raise someone strong, so they stop allowing weakness.

And all of it is done in the name of love, of virtue, of doing the right thing.

But the result is often the opposite, the child grows up fearful, disconnected, or ashamed of their real self. They do not feel guided. They feel corrected. They do not feel seen. They feel shaped. The parent was not abusive. They were convinced they were doing good. But the good hardened into pressure, and the pressure quietly turned into pain.

This is the danger of unchecked morality, not immorality. The kind that grows not from selfishness, but from a sense of righteousness that is too sure of itself to reflect.

The same thing happens in schools. Teachers who want to instill discipline might humiliate students who fall behind. Administrators who want to create safety might design rules that punish vulnerability. A school system that claims to care about growth might enforce a culture of fear, strict, measurable, always watching.

It becomes less about helping students thrive and more about controlling outcomes. The intention was good. The method strips out empathy. Students learn what to avoid, not what to explore.

In these cases, virtue becomes institutional, and once that happens, it becomes much harder to question. No one wants to challenge something that claims to be acting in the name of good.

But moral confidence at scale becomes bureaucracy. And bureaucracy, by nature, does not listen.

This paradox also shows up in personal relationships. A friend who is always correcting you. A partner who always thinks they know what is best for you. A mentor who offers advice but never asks questions. These people may care. Their concern may be real. But they stop offering presence and start offering correction. They stop hearing nuance and start issuing rules.

What began as support becomes control. What began as love becomes direction. And the more certain they are that their way is right, the more suffocating their goodness becomes.

The result is emotional distance, and in some cases, silent resentment. Because the person being "helped" is no longer a participant. They are now someone being managed.

And even when the help is rooted in good intention, the effect can feel like quiet domination.

The Principles That Destroy Peace

A rule can be right and still be wrong in the moment.

This is one of the most difficult truths for people who care about doing what is good. We are taught to believe that fairness, honesty, justice, and accountability are the foundations of peace. And often, they are. But what is rarely acknowledged is that even the most noble principles, when applied without reflection, can destroy the very peace they were meant to protect.

This is the paradox. Doing the right thing at the wrong time can become the reason things fall apart.

Not because the value was incorrect, but because it was unexamined, automatic, or delivered without care for the situation.

Imagine a group project. One person clearly does more work than the others. When the presentation ends, the teacher gives everyone the same grade. One student speaks up, demanding fairness, insisting that individual effort should be reflected in the score. The logic is solid. But the public confrontation embarrasses the group. It sparks resentment. It turns a quiet frustration into a visible conflict. The demand for fairness was not wrong. But the way it was expressed, in that moment, created more division than resolution.

The situation is not uncommon. Someone tries to correct a wrong and ends up creating a new one. Not because their principle was invalid, but because their approach ignored context.

You see this in workplaces where people insist on following rules exactly as written, even when doing so causes unnecessary harm. A manager denies a last-minute time-off request because it violates policy, even if the reason is personal and urgent. A teammate refuses to adjust a task because "that is not how we do it here." These responses defend structure, but they also reject humanity.

The result is not order. It is quite hostile. The principle becomes more important than the people it was supposed to serve.

Even fairness, when applied without flexibility, can backfire.

Consider a parent with two children. One breaks a rule by accident. The other does it on purpose. The parent, determined to be fair, gives both the same consequence. But instead of feeling respected, both children feel misunderstood. The one who made a mistake feels punished unfairly. The one who knew better feels falsely equal. The parent followed a principle, but lost trust in the process.

That is the hidden cost of applying values too rigidly. They can look just, but feel unjust. They can sound right, but land wrong.

This paradox becomes more visible the larger the system.

In law, fairness is often defined as consistency. Equal punishment for equal offenses. Predictable consequences. Structured response. These are the foundations of legal order. But rigid fairness can produce outcomes that feel deeply unfair. A first-time offender receives the same sentence as someone who has harmed repeatedly. A judge cannot make an exception because the law, in the name of equality, leaves no room for understanding.

In these moments, the principle of fairness holds, but justice does not land. What was meant to bring peace instead breeds quiet resentment and visible distrust. People do not reject the idea of law. They reject its inability to see what is human.

The rule was followed. The relationship was broken.

The same pattern exists in public discourse. A leader says something controversial. A journalist confronts them. The facts are correct. The accountability is justified. But the tone is combative, the timing poorly chosen. Supporters of the leader do not reflect on the issue. They dig in deeper. Not because they oppose truth, but because the way the truth was delivered felt like an attack.

The journalist followed the rules of their role. They insisted on integrity. But it was polarization.

The principle was right. The impact was damage.

This is the danger of moral automation. When someone holds a value, even a good one, and applies it without pausing to ask, "Is this the right moment? Is this the right method? What else is happening here?" then the value stops guiding. It starts pushing.

It creates more tension than it relieves.

And in its worst form, it gives the person applying it a false sense of superiority. Because they are doing what is "right," they feel entitled to ignore how their actions affect the people around them.

That is how peace collapses in places where everyone thinks they are being responsible.

The Belief That Cannot Be Questioned

Two people can pray to the same God, follow the same scripture, and live by the same code, and still see the world completely differently.

They will both say they are right. They will both believe they are faithful. But what they believe, deep down, is not identical. One sees discipline. The other sees love. One emphasizes punishment. The other sees redemption. One focuses on truth. The other focuses on mercy. Their rituals are the same. Their language overlaps. But their inner lives, what they mean when they say "I believe" — are not the same at all.

This is the paradox. The most unquestioned beliefs are often the least understood, even by the people who claim them.

Religion is one of the clearest places this plays out. Billions of people follow sacred texts, traditions, and prophets. They pray, gather, and live by moral structures handed down through generations. But even within the same religion, there are quiet fractures. Not just across denominations or sects, but between individuals. Two people raised under the same teachings can emerge with completely different convictions. One sees forgiveness as central. The other sees justice. One finds peace in obedience. The other finds it in questioning.

And yet each one believes they are following the truth.

Not a version of it. The truth.

What makes this so difficult to untangle is that no one can fully verify their version. There is no test that proves whose interpretation is correct. There is no moment when the belief becomes a fact. And still, people argue. People divide. People go to war over something they cannot prove, because what they feel is stronger than what they can show.

Faith is powerful not because it is confirmed, but because it does not need to be.

That is what makes this kind of division so unresolvable. It hides beneath agreement.

Two people may say the same words, quote the same verses, or defend the same tradition, and still live inside completely different beliefs. But because the language is shared, they assume the meaning is too. That assumption becomes dangerous.

When conflict arises, they are not just debating interpretation. They are accusing each other of abandoning the very foundation they both claim to stand on. But what is really happening is simpler, and stranger, they were never standing on the same thing to begin with.

They were just using the same vocabulary.

And as philosopher Blaise Pascal once wrote,

"We are usually convinced more easily by reasons we have found ourselves than by those which have occurred to others."

This is why two people can hear the same words, follow the same faith, and still diverge completely. Each person internalizes belief in a way that becomes deeply personal, shaped not by the original source, but by their own reflection in it. The belief feels objective, but it is built on subjective ground. It seems shared, but it is quietly singular.

That quote captures what centuries of disagreement often fail to explain: we are most loyal to the version of truth that feels like our own idea, even when we claim to follow something much larger than ourselves.

And that is the quiet contradiction beneath many shared beliefs. They appear united, but they are privately built. They claim one origin, but take a thousand shapes. And still, each person calls their shape the truth. Not because they are wrong, but because they have never seen how much of it they made themselves.

Final Note

This book is repetitive.

Not by accident, not out of laziness, and not because there was nothing new to say, but because the nature of paradox is repetition. It loops. It contradicts. It refuses to settle. You will hear the same conflict dressed in different languages. You will see the same structure in different subjects. You will feel as if the point has already been made. And then it will return again, through another lens, another example, another edge of the same shape.

That is not a flaw. That is the pattern of real life.

Paradoxes do not exist to be solved. They exist to be lived with. To be noticed, ignored, wrestled with, and repeated. You cannot escape them by thinking harder. You cannot defeat them by pretending they are not there. They come back, not always louder, but always deeper.

Control shows up in happiness. Truth shows up in identity. Belief bleeds into freedom. Every chapter is tied to the others, whether or not it says so directly. That is how contradiction works. It does not divide neatly. It blurs.

So if this book has felt circular, if some parts sounded familiar, if you wondered whether a chapter repeated what came before, you are not wrong.

That is exactly what it was meant to do.

Some things need to be said more than once to be understood at all.

About Me

I have always been drawn to contradictions, not as puzzles to be solved, but as truths that refuse to sit quietly. This book came from years of watching how people think, how systems work, and how often we live inside ideas that quietly undo themselves. The more I noticed, the harder it became to look away.

The Paradox Theory is not a set of lessons. It is not here to simplify life or hand out advice. It is a collection of tensions that I believe are worth sitting with. Some of them are frustrating. Some are uncomfortable. All of them are real. I wrote this book because I wanted to understand things more honestly, even if that meant accepting answers that were messy or incomplete.

I am a high school student. Some people assume that serious thinking only begins in adulthood, but that is not true. Seeing what is broken does not require a degree. You do not need decades of experience to know when something is off. Clarity is not earned through age. It is reached through attention. Anyone can see what matters, no matter how young they are, once they stop trying to fit into the version of life they were handed.

This book was not written from a place of expertise. It was written from curiosity, and from the feeling that something deeper is always sitting beneath what we accept as normal. I wanted to ask better questions. I wanted to look at the patterns we live by but never name. That is where this started.

If you made it this far, then I hope something in these pages stayed with you, even if just one sentence, one idea, or one contradiction that you will never see the same way again.

www.ingramcontent.com/pod-product-compliance
Lightning Source LLC
Chambersburg PA
CBHW060152050426
42446CB00013B/2780